JOURNEY
Beyond Despair

JOURNEY
Beyond Despair

A MEMOIR OF
LOVE,
PSYCHOSIS,
AND THE
POWER OF INSIGHT

Julie Howard Parker

Cerulean 🐝 Publications
Altadena, CA
2025

Journey Beyond Despair: A Memoir of Love, Psychosis, and the Power of Insight

Published by Cerulean ⚘ Publications, Altadena, California
journey@juliehowardparker.com
www.juliehowardparker.com

ISBN (paperback): 979-8-9920605-0-8
ISBN (ebook): 979-8-9920605-1-5
ISBN (hardcover): 979-8-9920605-2-2
Audio download ISBN: 979-8-9920605-3-9

Book design and production by www.AuthorSuccess.com
Cover art by www.istock.com
Writing Bluebird design, Clare Walker Leslie
Author photo by Dirk Bolle

Printed in the United States of America

Library of Congress Control Number: 2025902180

For permissions or to schedule a reading, talk or discussion, visit the author's website: juliehowardparker.com
For Free Questionnaire, "Do You Know the Story your Life is Telling You?" visit the author's website, www.juliehowardparker.com

Permission has been obtained to quote from Jerry Stahl, *Nein, Nein, Nein!*

This memoir is not intended as a substitute for medical advice. The reader should consult a physician in all matters of health, particularly mental/emotional health. Theories about lives other than the author's life are explorations only, included to increase compassion for human suffering.

To Peter and our family,
with love and gratitude

When I looked in the mirror,
the mask of my enemy fell off.

Contents

Introduction

Every spring, like migrating birds, Peter and I, wedded for seven decades, close up our tile-roofed Mediterranean home and abandon Southern California. We are headed across the country to rural Vermont, where our forestry life awaits us. There are not many years left for us to repeat this pattern. Most of our cohort–siblings, friends, neighbors–have fallen by the wayside. We are survivors, solid on our feet for ninety-year-olds.

As we drive along on the two-lane country asphalt, Peter at the wheel of our rented Kia, I study his profile outlined against the open window. His chiseled chin is still strong and crows' feet still crinkle when he smiles. I hardly notice the paling blue of his eyes, the hollows beneath them, the lines of weariness. I reach over and smooth his silver hair lopping into a cowlick A breeze wafts in, erasing Los Angeles from our nostrils.

Vermont! The land where we met, the ridge where our woods roads will beckon us to head up the rise hand in hand once again. We make a left turn onto our gravel road. In four miles we see the big pine looming ahead. There it is, our 1840s white-shuttered red farmhouse. The lawn is newly mown to the woods' edge. Neighbors take care of us, turning on the electricity and trapping mice. Our children and grandchildren with their toddlers will come visit us. My heart dances.

But it has not always danced. Oh no, it has not always.

This very farmhouse is the scene of my last major episode of a mental illness that tore our family apart episodically. Now, I can look back upon that forty-year period as if it were someone else's calamity, laced with terror and shame. I could not have written this memoir with such frank detail at the age of fifty, sixty or even seventy. Nor could my insight have matured enough to draw certain conclusions. It is, in fact, due to the long arc of years, from age twenty when my first symptoms erupted, to age eighty when I finally began recording them, that I recognized the chain of unfolding events as archetypal. In Jungian terms, this suggests an eternal pattern that holds meaning for all human beings. Who are we all? What factors decide the nature of our individual journeys?

I came into this world a passionate, high-spirited little kid. When provoked, I flashed a fiery temperament. Most of the time, however, I escaped into fantasy. There, my self-appointed role was to protect victims, long-suffering and noble, besieged by wickedness. Entering the nightly trauma caused by a troubled mother, I became Snow White, stalked by the queen in the telltale wall mirror. It was I who was offered that poisoned apple. Cinderella in rags was really Julie, sweeping the hearth. From my earliest memories, I searched for my ideal—safety, kindness, generosity, dependability. In my five-year-old mind, fairytales helped me survive a bewildering and scary family life.

This early facility for slipping into the lead role of childhood fables has been influential to this day. When I sat down twelve years ago to search for deeper meaning in the trauma of our young married years, I spotted the major stages making up the journey that all of us are traveling. Oddly, the more treacherous the path, the more illuminating the final goal may be.

So, we are about to go back in time. I choose to begin this story at the end of a period that has highly intoxicated me, true to my porous nature. It has turned the darkness of post-war Europe into an exciting world of my own creation. The act of leaving it behind is about to pull us into perilous territory.

Never lose touch, however, with the fact that Peter and I, in great health today, loving life and each other more deeply *due to this story*, are at peace in our world. Time knows us well. With only a handful of years left, carrying Neptune Society cards in our wallets, we sleep long, eat well and delight in endless interests, especially our daughters' and grandchildren's lives. My hope, as you read along with me, is that this tale will inspire your unique journey and that you, too, may experience, if you glimpse and confront your own hidden trickster-parts, the wonder of what I name, simply, Arrival.

PART ONE
Detroit and Chicago
1952-1963

Running until she can run no longer, Julie crosses the threshold into the living horror of psychosis and a battle against self-annihilation. Scenes in the psychiatric hospital alternate with flashbacks to early family life, her tense ordinary world. A fierce little dreamer seeks ideals, omnipotence.

I

Running

I would not recognize the student I once was in Paris if, on a return visit to the 1950s, I saw her rush past me, books slipping, hair flying, to catch the open-backed green bus grinding its way toward the Boulevard St. Germain. We would mean nothing to each other, she, late to class in her camel's hair coat with the hem flapping loose, I headed toward the apartment she had just left. But if I did not glance back to watch her swing up onto that crowded platform, the whole meaning of a life might be lost.

Luckily, there is always a thread, maybe dangling from that coat lining needing mending. Only memory can tie it against unraveling. The thread is powerful, but so are the forces that will do all they can, as this story unfolds, to undo it. Oblivious, there I am, at the outset, sailing into a sea of blankness on a vessel that hides my fate . . .

From the gently rocking deck of the great ocean liner, only moments earlier I had been gazing absently at the blue-black gloss of the vast Atlantic. A gloom of fog blanketed the red and black funnels of the RMS Queen Mary. Smoke trailed behind us, flecking its soot above the sprawling wake. I had said farewell to the year 1953, one of pessimism in postwar Europe. The ship, recently refitted from troop transport to peacetime travel, was bearing me homeward from a college year abroad.

Life, mine at least, was churning along with that giant steel hull over the waters of my own unconscious. France was fading behind, its shores no longer visible. The horizon ahead was a filament of nothingness. I was swaying between two worlds.

Inspiration had carried me here. Study abroad was unusual in 1952, but I had fidgeted in French class under sterile noun declensions until an idea—*exchange student!*—had altered the future of my major. France would spirit me away to an exotic, thrilling continent. Peter and I, as deeply in love as we were that year at Middlebury College, had agreed after endless vacillating that I should go. I had toned down my excitement, picturing him longing for me, my faithful steady, on the snowbound Vermont campus. He would be waiting for me in Chicago.

Now, floating between two landmasses without a toehold in either, I entered hazardous water. Suddenly, a knifelike jolt, followed by a sense of dread, rose up from somewhere inside me. I froze, sensing danger. It was as if an element of my mind had just cracked, allowing in something unknown, intent on harm. Instinctively, I pushed down, running in fright from this threat out of nowhere.

What had just happened? I was trying to picture greeting Peter, after so many months apart. I looked around. Nothing had changed in my surroundings—the murky salt water was still chopping and peaking. A new wave surged, bursting upward, widening the fissure. Was some membrane that shielded my normal world giving way? I felt a strange unmooring, as if the "who I am" had ruptured. Leaking out through that crack was the only "me" I knew. And flooding in was a force distinctly threatening.

Panting, I looked for something to hold on to. When another upthrust rocked my whole being, my heart pounded wildly. I swayed as if stepping into quicksand. My legs buckled.

The assault subsided temporarily. My thoughts raced. Was this ship's destination the cause of this peril, steaming me back to a life I'd outgrown?

A new surge pushed through the fissure like lava. Something abnormal was definitely taking place, overpowering the vowels and rhythms of two languages colliding in my brain. I staggered. All the rich and novel ways of seeing life from a war-torn perspective were shattering. The love I was trying to retain for Peter was oozing into a limbo.

I clutched the barrier edging the deck and glanced around, fearing others could see what was happening. Objects, people, and distances now played tricks on my focus. A man in a black coat a few yards away stared into the horizon, tapping his cigarette ashes. When he turned my way, I shrank, pretending to dig into my purse for glasses. I backed away from the painted iron rungs of the railing. Concealing my panic, I smiled at deck strollers, waving and nodding mechanically. At dinner time, I faked a laugh at a table mate's fatuous gags, then excused myself before dessert. I was now pushing constantly against something deadly no one could see inside me. Like a malignancy, it was feeding upon its host, a student named Julie.

That evening, my nerves chaperoned every step I took to avoid plunging down the narrow metal stairs to my tiny bunk room. The lowest deck throbbed with the roar of the ship's engines as the acrid smell of fuel permeated the long corridor leading to my cubicle. Inside the cramped cell, I climbed into the narrow bed and lay awake under a thin blanket. All night long, dreading where sleep might take me, I listened to the muffle of the giant propellers turning in the boiler room with my heaving heart, chanting *"horrroom . . . horrroom . . . horrroom."*

The next morning, I arose in this same terrified state, pushing, pushing against the alien force that was threatening my survival. Four chilling words emerged, marking the end of my enchanted French year:

I'm losing my mind. Where was I headed? How would I function once I landed? Panic had not yet destroyed my reasoning.

Peter! I shuddered, trying to reconstruct his face. I hadn't seen him since his Christmas visit to Paris, where, in a sidewalk café, I had confessed guilt to him that my feelings had wandered briefly to a fellow student. We parted after that vacation with our trust in one another shaken. Was that the source of this distortion? A week earlier I had been running to catch the underground metro, hurrying back to Madame Girard's for the main meal at noon, juggling courses expertly in a language that was rivaling my own. I had soared, almost giddy. My very pores were saturated with foreign ways of doing things.

A scarier thought now surfaced. Might this "happening," this weird, enemy force sucking me downward, rise from something so twisted that I would join the corridors of the incurable? The ship's foghorn blew its mournful warning. I continued pushing down with all my strength, running from my own legs.

The great Cunard liner was cruising closer and closer to the Port of New York where Peter and I had said our tearful goodbyes a year earlier. A memory surfaced of my waving to him from above on the massive ship deck, he on the platform below, receding. I was returning a ghost of that extroverted, vibrant me, playful despite my hair too oily, forehead dotted with pimples. He didn't care about any of these blemishes, loving only my easy laughter, my lightheartedness. Fearing his rejection of a girlfriend so altered, I began scheming about how I could hide from him, postpone our reunion in the hope the symptoms might fade.

There is no turning around an eighty-thousand-ton ocean liner. It was conveying me back a stranger to everything I had left behind. My mind whirled with one crazy thought: how to gain time, avoid meeting the one I feared losing. Peter, the fulfillment of the ideal I had sought all through a wobbly childhood! I could not let him find me. His presence might save me if I escaped from him. When we first met, our magnetism rocketed us into the space where legends launch. I was his capricious sprite. He was my rock, earthbound, reliable, wise.

On the last night aboard ship, desperate thoughts took hold of me. What were my options? Should I end my life right there, silently, unobserved, in my tiny room among the 500 lowest class cubby holes on D deck? But wait. Wouldn't that act deprive me of a chance at maturity, at adulthood, no matter how harrowing? The attainment of that beautiful state of fulfillment had been my dream since childhood. Shouldering the yoke of responsibility, of pulling my weight beside my partner, was the goal that drove me but terrified me. There was no way out. When we landed, I phoned my closest friend, Diane. She had taken a counselor position at the remote Vermont camp we had loved as teenagers. They needed a tennis counselor.

Months after stepping off that ship, managing to elude Peter for a little while, I had grown accustomed to the husk I had become. I was getting the hang of pushing down against my pursuer. It required all my life force to be directed inward. But when Peter and I finally connected, as the camp season ended, he hardly noticed a change. His welcoming smile crinkled the corners of his ocean-blue eyes. His long firm embrace, his obvious relief to have me at his side, gave me courage to continue masquerading as normal.

All through that final year of college, I clung to my faithful senior. Peter interpreted my neediness as a culture clash. Pushing down had become a habit. In class, lectures and dialogue muffled the menace until the bell rang. I glued my arm to Peter's as we studied in the library. Focusing fiercely upon class assignments, I dared not let up, or the monster might geyser, demolishing our future.

We graduated with diplomas in our two specialties, French and philosophy, and married—Peter in contentment, I in a split reality.

Slowly, I adapted to fear and intense sorrow over the Julie I once was. I told no one what I was feeling inside, not even Peter. While he served hated years as a draftee in the Army, my simple presence sustained him. He lived with his own insecurity during that final phase of the Korean War. The birth of three daughters offered me some affirmation, even if the first was followed by postpartum symptoms of a new, hair-raising variety. I loved motherhood. My vivacity returned a little. Perhaps I was slowly healing. Then it happened.

2

Accepting the Abyss, 1960

Icy winds hurled their barbs in a westward sweep over Lake Michigan, playing the clapboards of our sturdy starter home like a zither. I had just turned twenty-eight, a mother with three tiny children, one a newborn, in our white-trimmed two-story cape, cozy against the howling bitterness outside. After all that trudging from one southern Army base to another, it was our family nest at last, in a transitional sector of Chicago's neighboring Hinsdale. At the Singer, I was sewing the seams of a tiny pair of corduroy overalls. I focused in front of me as the whirring of the feeder blended with Diane and Katherine at my feet, chattering, scattering blocks and books around the living room. Celeste was asleep upstairs in her cradle.

Our white picket fence edged busy York Road, where traffic slushed down the slope toward Ogden Avenue, a crass necklace of used car lots, collision centers, and auto parts shops. Peter was at work, having driven off after the usual five minutes of scraping ice from the windshield in our driveway. One day we might build a garage. I had waved to him, smiling through the front window. Mental illness, it appeared, was behind me, thanks to a year of psychotherapy in Detroit after the birth of my first daughter, Diane. Prior symptoms, erupting as I returned

9

from a student year in France, had subsided. Dr. Warren had initiated me into the mysteries of psychology and early childhood relationships, especially mother-daughter ones. Peter had been mystified, stalwart, and as dismayed as I over my postpartum visions so unspeakable that, disintegrating, I had jumped on an emergency flight homeward with my newborn, eight weeks old. My parents, one a doctor at the Henry Ford Hospital, had located the analyst. Dr. Max Warren had helped me focus on surface topics until those bludgeoning visions slowly evaporated.

My artful management of our growing household pleased me, even causing a little smugness. It was time to give up my therapy with Dr. Billford, whom Dr. Warren had suggested as a replacement analyst in the Chicago area. Dr. Billford, hardly older than I was, made me uncomfortable with his silences, his wavy dark hair, penetrating eyes, and goatee. He looked too much like my older brother whom I had worshipped, but who had spurned me in grade school. Sessions with him led into risky territory I could not talk about.

"Don't you hate your kids at times?"

It was my neighbor, Edith Whipple in tears on our porch, hair in curlers. I invited her in as a below-zero gust shoved against our front door, ushering in her tots, sniffling and wiping runny noses with mittens.

"I know what you mean," I lied. Our daughters made me proud in their matching outfits designed on my Singer. They charmed diners at nearby tables in the Toll Road restaurant as cars whizzed by beneath. I loved watching their unique personalities bud. The visiting siblings pouted as their mother snapped at them for fingering the tinsel on the balsam tree sagging in the corner.

"How about hot cocoa?" I suggested, and breezed into the kitchen in hostess mode.

Edith followed me, sullen. My mothering skills shone in comparison to hers. But exhaustion was increasing for me too as tiny Celeste awoke night after night for feedings. Christmas had come and gone. The tree decorations drooped. Branches rained needles all over the half-read Beatrix Potter tales. The boots of our little visitors kicked Peter Rabbit about, bending pages, leaving melting puddles on the rug. We had a tea party in our new extension, with its unfinished walls creating a hall and third bedroom. It smelled of wet plaster. Edith left, unconsoled.

"Diane? Shall we take a ride down to the new drive-in on Ogden Avenue and get a hamburger for lunch?" Diane was my miniature buddy, out of diapers.

Diane rushed for her boots. She loved that tiny spot squeezed between car lots. You could whiff the sizzling patties before you caught sight of the golden arches. I felt slightly guilty, greasy burgers for a three-year-old, newborn baby Celeste in arms, and Katherine just learning to talk. Never mind. I loved my trio of little beauties who resembled their handsome father. And I was efficient . . . the perfect homemaker in the kitchen with apples, frozen peas and a can of tuna.

But my milk was drying up. And with it would go something heady about childbirth: voluptuous breasts, the brief fun of playing Earth Mother, nourishing all the planet's offspring. I was shrinking back to my flat-chested, sexless body that had never quite left childhood.

It began on that same bleak January afternoon of our trip to McDonald's, with dusk approaching. As I passed the dining room archway of our new addition to warm up a bottle and fetch a bib for Celeste, a sudden bolt ripped through my brain. Instantly I froze, remembering. "No!" I felt a titan force inside my mind pull me into peril. "Again?" I clasped my temples and staggered a moment, heart racing, scalp prickling. A metallic taste of raw fear spread from tongue to nostrils. I steadied myself, crying out to the living room walls, now closing in. Terror flooded up through the old fissure in my consciousness.

The moment passed. I perched, panting, on the edge of the southern pine couch we had brought north from our Army years in Georgia. Suddenly, everything ordinary and safe—living room, children playing on the rug, Peter at work, York Road out front, cars heading home-ward—retreated. My vision shrank. The walls contracted. Getting up unsteadily, I walked back and forth, pacing past the entrance leading to our new downstairs bedroom. Celeste was fussing in the hallway upstairs between the two bedrooms we'd now outgrown.

A new assault, more deadly than the first, tore like a tsunami through my prickling brain. It swept me from children, furniture, walls, scatter-ing us like flotsam. I clung to a chair, staggered to a door frame. The force was colossal, like a black hole sucking me downward, into what felt like time and space swirling into a bottomless funnel. I was slipping into shock. Something much more lethal than all my past symptoms was spinning me into its void. It was yanking me loose from Earth, from Peter, and from our three unsuspecting little ones.

My entire body now trembled. I was losing the battle with this inner menace. Mechanically I warmed the bottle, carried it back upstairs to the baby and functioned as mother of three until Peter returned, the man I loved. I heard his boots stomp on the porch. As he came through the front door, he sensed something was wrong. His smile died.

"I've had a new episode. A really scary one." I searched his eyes as I stepped toward him. "What, again?" Peter tried to fathom what he was hearing as he took off his gloves and heavy coat and stopped. Tall, angular, wearing his oxford blue shirt and tan khakis, he scrutinized me. At dinner, our eyes searched the walls in opposite directions.

"I've got to make a decision." My mind was feverishly talking with itself.

"But I thought you had learned how to handle—"

"There is no way out for me, Peter . . . trying to resist by pushing down is only a stopgap. Running to therapists doesn't work. It only fools me into thinking I'm better. This force keeps returning. I've got to face it."

"Face it . . . how?"

"I don't know. I just cannot run from it any longer."

I saw myself deliberately turning around, slowly, consciously, choosing, with no other option, to yield to that force, and to let it pull me into its gaping abyss. Seeing no way out, I accepted my extinction. Everything in that moment, on that evening, tore apart all we lived for.

I helped put the children to bed and lay down in limbo. I had no idea what would happen next. At 3 a.m., as little Celeste woke up with the familiar whimpering, I descended the stairs to warm her bottle. On the way back through the living room, I passed out on the green rug our in-laws had lent us. Peter heard the bottle roll across the floor.

"Julie?" he called out in the darkness. When there was no answer, he rushed downstairs and found me lifeless. He dialed Dr. Billford, who answered groggily.

"Phone me in the morning. I think we'd better admit her to a hospital for a couple of weeks."

I came to, got back into bed and hallucinated for the rest of the night. In my vision I lay on a white clinical hospital bed. Doctors stood in a circle all around threatening to kill me. The vision seemed inspired by Rembrandt's early painting, a small print of which had always hung on my pediatrician father's den wall. In it, a physician, Dr. Nicolaes Tulp, was instructing medical students in seventeenth-century anatomy using a corpse stretched out on a table before them. As a child, I had shivered at the picture.

The next morning Dr. Billford made the arrangements for my admission to Forest Hospital, a private psychiatric facility on the banks of the Des Plaines River in a county wilderness preserve. "She'll probably be there only for a week or two," he reassured Peter.

I was already slipping from ordinary reality.

Peter's mind whirled. His life, my life, our lives were headed into chaos. Maryanne Snowfield next door hurried over to stay with our children for an hour or two as he drove me to the hospital. Next, he called work and then his widowed father to say he would bring our daughters to his country spot, the home Peter had grown up in nearby, once I was admitted. Nancy, the housekeeper, could help for a day while he made a general plan.

My last memory of a tie to the home that had seemed so full of happy tots and maternal competence died on that drive to the asylum. We didn't speak. I was halfway into my own underworld. At the reception desk, I remember a woman asking, "Who is going to sign Mrs. Parker in?" I responded with a last thread of pride, "I'm signing myself in." I was given an evaluation test, asking for meanings to several adages like "A stitch in time saves nine," and got stuck on "Strike while the iron is hot." Vexed, I scribbled all over the paper. From that moment on, the "I" that was "me," that put on clothes, or put a spoon to mouth or put the right name to mother, father, husband and children, unraveled to a tiny thread-like filament. Even that thread was being reeled in by a force known only to the severely mentally ill.

3

The Eye and the Bloody Axe

The Forest Hospital attendant guided me to a yellow cinder-block room on the first floor with two single beds and a roommate in her mid-seventies. He showed me the closet, where I hung up the few clothes packed that morning, and a shelf, upon which I set my beautiful box of Crane stationery. It contained not only ivory vellum writing sheets but a pearly blue fountain pen newly filled with ink. Why had I packed them?

I had the vague sense of a hallway stretching down an endless corridor with doorways into cheerless, clinical rooms.

The small, independent psychiatric hospital had a high chain-link fence surrounding its frontage on the Des Plaines River. The doors to the lounge and ward were locked. Forest Hospital, as I look back, could be considered a "safe place apart for those too disturbed to function," and for as long as a patient needed, with 125 beds set up a little like low-cost college dormitories built in the 1950s, rectangles without frills.[1] I was vaguely aware of being led to my cubicle and then back to the main salon.

---

1. My illness predated the era of patients' rights, the Affordable Care Act, and the unlawfulness of retaining any disturbed person for more than a "72-hour hold." Private psychiatric hospitals like Forest would close one by one.

Feeling myself contracting, yet at the same time being blasted apart, I sat on a chair in the lounge, mummy-like. I crunched my shoulders, with my eyes closed and head squeezed into my neck cavity. I didn't move. When it was dinner time someone said, "Come on Julie, we'll show you where the dining room is." Dining room? Eat? One doesn't eat where I was, one holds oneself. I was pulled up out of the chair and led stumbling down a scary tunnel to a table and a chair. I ate nothing, sitting exactly as I had in the lounge. A few patients appeared to be chattering senselessly.

A part of my mind, squashed by galactic forces, was observing what was happening. An "I", inseparable from the individual that makes me "me," was being subjected to a current too powerful for any human. Some "membrane" in normal consciousness had cracked or given way in my psyche. Through this fissure, I now felt forces sucking me downward, backward, spiraling into a treacherous void. My brain, in cold terror, could feel itself being spun dizzyingly through this dread tunnel into the great, undifferentiated pull of time regressing backward toward the Big Bang. The elements of space-time had broken into me, allowing the whole of our species' evolution to flood in, to dissolve my separateness. I clung to that observing "I," as if a thread existed between the two, "I" and "me." Where that thread originated was beyond human ken, perhaps its source arose out of all I had experienced and cognitively acquired in my twenty-eight years since birth. But it did exist. The "I" that saw, that watched, was also the "I" that could have been written "Eye." Was there some kind of relationship between the two? The sounds of our spoken words play mysterious tricks on our ears. Furthermore, that I or Eye had a shape, and a persistent place. It was a black dot, never disappearing, watching me. In the swirling infinity, terror was my only constant except for that piercing point of blackness. It called to my awareness because it was there, a kind of companion in that emptiness, a presence I could count upon. With this Eye or black dot observing, I now sank into an alien universe, hopeless and annihilating. Home as a concept had dissolved. My "I-ness" had been effaced to a zero, an aught, a hole in space where Julie once existed. Only the Eye, the black point, remained, observing.

Since Dr. Billford did not work with hospitalized patients, he had referred me to Dr. Lacroix, a small, roundish man with shiny dark hair slicked back as though pomaded, above an expressionless face despite staring eyes. His job was probably to check on me weekly, diagnose my illness, track my progress and come up with a treatment plan. But I clung to Dr. Billford simply because he was familiar, and a connection to regularly scheduled appointments in his office when I was emerging from depression. His visit was important to me. He came that first week. I still held a faint imprint of the outside world and knew my distorted mind was in another place. We sat in the open lounge.

"I am never going to get out of here." My head, bent toward my knees, may have unnerved the analyst used to patients in armchair settings glancing at him now and then. "I am lost. I know that this is the end of me."

"My, you are terribly gloomy. What makes you so negative and bleak?" The analyst added, "I can't understand what has come over you to be so without hope."

Not only had Dr. Billford failed to say something helpful; he chose words that reinforced what terrified me. With no further exchange, he made a hurried exit. Now, the psychotic dimension of what would be the norm for my illness set in in earnest.

There I am in the lounge, oblivious to others, feeling my skull turn inside out like raw flesh. My own mind is electrocuting me. I call out but my voice fails. "Help! God! Somebody! I can smell my brain cells on fire! This is death alive, inferno!"

These overloads come and go, electric bolts from neuron to synapse of such force that they leave in their wake an image of a charred braincase.

My body wraps itself, arms tight to ribs, neck drawn in turtle-like, fetal. Then follows a different horror, a repeating gory massacre so real that even now, as I describe it, my scalp prickles. I see, I feel, a huge steel-gray axe over my head. It is like something out of a medieval dungeon. It descends powerfully into my skull, splitting me in two. I run screaming across the room, clutching my temples. The force of the impact, the feel of the cutting blade, gash me apart. The scene passes. I pant, gasping. A nurse comes to me, patting my shoulder. I have made it through the bludgeoning until it comes again.

Though psychosis was unleashing a savagery upon me, and my mind was creating torture instruments, I still sensed the ever-present Eye watching. I was floating in astral space like a lost bit of consciousness. Yet that indelible speck of blackness was always there. What was it doing? Why was it watching, never absent for a second, appearing to be interested? It did not intervene, it simply observed. I held my fragmented self together, sitting without stirring, like a landmine ready to explode at the first foot grazing it. I could not wiggle. I hovered between imploding, collapsing into an endless undertow dragging me backward, and detonating outward with such a psychic blast my atoms might scatter irretrievably.

By the fifth week, I was still sitting in the lounge with arms wrapping my ribs mummy-like. Dr. Lacroix approached and guided me to a small counseling room for a first consultation. He had decided to continue a semblance of psychotherapy because Dr. Warren, my Detroit analyst, had reported I responded positively to it. In this tiny enclosure, the physician appeared far away in his armchair, down a long burrow separating us. He watched me, saying nothing. Then I spoke.

"Do you see any progress in me?" The question showed a shred of awareness that two of us were in that room, that wellness was present as a concept.

"No." Dr. Lacroix stated simply. Then he turned the question around. "Do you?"

"Yes," I said.

"Oh? What do you see?"

At that point, chin sunk, eyes shuttered, knees drawn upward in womb position, with my left index finger I drew an image in the space in front of my chest. It was of a winding path. I made a few little turns back and forth with that finger, picturing a "me" inching along a trail beginning at the foot of a steep incline whose summit was lost in the stratosphere. I whispered, "I am traveling up a mountain. I have started. I have gone this far." Dr. Lacroix said nothing. If he raised his eyebrows I did not see it. I did not, but surely the Eye did.

If John, the mystical fourth Evangelist, was right in launching his Gospel with "In the beginning was the Word," which Eastern spirituality interprets as vibration, sound, and gives the Sanskrit translation, "Aum" or "Om," might not that Word in our English language be translated as "I," or "Eye," or even "Aye," saying yes to life? Why did that Eye, that black point that never disappeared throughout those early months in psychosis, appear to me when I was lost in Infinity, torn from my tiny carapace of Julie on Earth, now floating anchorless among the galaxies?

What was its role, its raison d'être . . . this never-ending Eye observing me? Looking back sixty years later, I feel intense interest in this Observer. Observing is a faculty; a stone does not have such a faculty. An intelligence has the faculty of observing. And if the Observer is an intelligence, it suggests there is an operating principle, a reason why the Observer is observing. This statement could be endlessly argued. However, my disorder stripped away the swathing blinding normal humanity to the fact we are being observed.

Though extremely dangerous, mental illness can give a star-tling advantage to the psychotic if the psychotic is willing to explore where the observing is leading.

To my curiosity's surprise, as I pondered, while writing and reviewing still-vital memories from decades ago, this observing entity playfully slipped into two aspects: the stoic and the sympathizer. Joining this narrative insistently, the two have taken on names as they converse: Daemon and Cerulean Fairy. Their conversation shows they have something in mind for me—for all humans. They want to mark turning points, to record my journey in their way, not mine, in their Cosmic Log. In this story, the two will visit off and on, and dialogue.

4

Triangle, 1939

I am traveling back in time to our home in Highland Park, Michigan, peeking in on those first years of childhood. There it is, number 142 California Street, our row house of brick and shingles squeezed between its neighbors, separated by wire fences sagging under honeysuckle vines. It is about 5 p.m. on a typical evening of my seventh or eighth year. I am standing next to Mother. She is pacing wildly in the vestibule, a little square entry with coat hooks on three sides. We are waiting to greet my father, who is returning from a day with his patients. Three or four minutes have elapsed; the woman beside me is frantic, her vocal cords leaking throttled bits of sound. Something poisonous has come over her, as it does every night. Here is how it seemed to me at that age:

"Mommy is fun all day long until the sun sets. Then, she grows a horn. We hear steps on the porch, the doorknob turns and Daddy appears. He has his usual loving smile, in his dark wool coat smelling of wet snow, and hat that makes him handsome. He hangs it on its special hook. As he hugs me, because my arms stretch out to greet him, Mommy lashes out, her whining louder and softer.

"Where have you been! I'm beside myself waiting! The dinner is almost cold! Everything is nearly ruined!" Mommy's face is twitching more than usual. She sounds like she hates Daddy. I feel sad for him.

"Hi, Daddy!" I greet him, all happy. "Hi, Jule!" He has a voice like music. He gives a little lift on his toes like a shiver and glances at Mommy's frown. We hurry to the dining room. I love him. Oh, how I love him. He's smiling for me alone, for sure. Wouldn't any daddy returning home like the small welcoming arms more than the scary face? He's shrinking, poor Daddy. I want to rescue him. I'm afraid. He's afraid too, I can tell.

"It's like this night after night! I just feel miserable, no one cares!"

Daddy responds. "We all care! We're all trying to help you." Daddy is kind, but Mommy points a dagger at him.

"Don't line up the whole family against me like that!"

Now I'm scared. She might stab me, too."

As this frenzy continues, my father jumps around nervously, trying again. "Yes, Issie, I'm here now Issie. Let's sit right down to the table, everything will be fine . . ."

At the long, rectangular dining room table, my brothers and I each take our place in the blanket of tension. George, two years older, squirms more than sits at one end alone. Seeking crumbs of attention, I secretly long for his affection. Among his gang of buddy admirers, he calls out to me, always trailing behind him on the way to school, "Sissy, sissy, sissy! Too bad you're just a girl."

The neighborhood kids look up to him, with his swaggering confidence and piercing eyes alert for someone to taunt. He is a troublemaker in class, but so quick to finish the assignments without error that he cows his teachers. Jay, three years younger than I, sits at the other end as far from George as the table length permits. The boys make squeaking sounds to cut the tension. I giggle in support, but my mom turns to me and snaps my lips with her third finger pushing against her thumb. This strange little reprimand reminds me I am on her side. Indeed, I am. She and I sit next to each other alone on our table length across from my father. But I don't *want* to be her ally, a female I don't trust pitted against the males. My dad faces us, in front of the stack of plates and silver carving knife. My mom broods, waiting for the carving to begin.

On cue the skit begins, my father speaking the first lines. "Oh, this looks wonderful! Roast beef. It smells marvelous!"

"Issie, does this look about right for you?" (She accepts her plate sullenly while her husband serves the rest of us.)

"Jule?" He hands me a plate.

We wait for our mother to take the first bite and utter her first line.

"Oh, it tastes like sawdust! I worked so hard on it!"

"Why, it's wonderful! It is just perfect. It carves like a dream," my father chirps.

My brothers chime in, "It tastes great, Mom."

We want our mom to be happy so we can be happy. Even George, whose fiery temper no one can control, seems caught by the misery spinning its nightly web around all of us. It keeps us focused on our maternal parent, winding us in from its center. As we steal glances at each other, she picks at her dinner, pushing a bite away from her lips in a pique, asking one of the boys if they would like the rest of her serving.

Later in adolescence, I observed Mother's gift for ensnaring admirers. She had heady literary charms. I can see her now arching her eyebrows, rolling her eyes suggestively, referring to something vaguely erotic. My father, a deep romantic, had fallen for this femme fatale as an innocent evangelical from the Northfield, Massachusetts town of Dwight Moody's religious revival campus. He was "binaried" to his Isabell, calling her Issie adoringly in his Valentine's Day ditties. Where these nightly frenzies came from, neither he nor we children had any idea, nor probably did Mother, their victim.

Like a chameleon, our maternal parent bewildered our early years, switching from one persona to another. She delighted us and the neighborhood kids in daylight with an endless string of games and inventions. Friends wanted to play at our house where Mrs. Howard made it fun. I was proud of her. But with the fall of dusk, this complex woman segued into torment, baffling her three children, as well as our father. What was causing this misery? With darkness, Mother's face twitches accelerated. Her nerves frayed. She began to jerk her head and cast her eyes around wildly, on the offense, looking possessed. Sometimes these spells would last into the next afternoon for the poor woman. At age eight or nine, I glimpsed her one day twisting this way and that, half-crazy, in front of her bedroom mirror tearing at her hair, sobbing out vitriol at her image, "*Oh, I am so ugly, so ugly, so UGLY!*" This was the same mother who enchanted us all at holidays, making our Christmases and Halloweens so magical that our grade school buddies crowded around the front door to get invited in. They loved Mrs. Howard.

One particular Christmas was the turning point in my fragile longing for how Mother could sprinkle miracle dust. That night and morning will never die, even though it preceded my Great Disillusionment . . .

"*Tu sais cette poupée . . .*" I catch the magical sound of the phrase "Père Noël" as my mother chats about a doll with my father, preparing for Christmas. She has been in a honeyed humor, whispering secrets in French to my father. Strange utterings opening doors to enchanted worlds, accessories for Mommy the enchantress. Tonight will be Christmas Eve. Spirits bubble. The whole family is relaxed and smiling, even George. The table is fragrant with balsam and pine greens winding in an oval around flickering red tapers. Within reach, reigning in the center, our German music box spins as little angels on a wooden platform circle around Mary and baby Jesus. I make it play Silent Night over and over.

Dinner is finally finished, uneaten peas forgiven on the plate. I am handed the candle snuffer and carefully lower it four times, turning flames to pungent smoke trails. The moment has come. Everyone follows the sorceress in command into the living room by the fireplace. We three children—my two brothers and I—bend over a short-legged table by the hearth, engrossed in an act of magic. We have arranged the doily and butter plate in the center of the polished wood surface with two homemade cookies. The blue Shirley Temple pitcher is filled with milk. Now we compose, with our mother's orchestration, a letter to Santa.

"How do you spell 'locomotive'?"

That's my younger brother Jay. He is Mother's pet, and runs home crying every time Davie Crowley picks on him, playing rough on purpose. I wouldn't deign to seek such sissy cuddling. But tonight all is bright and calm. And safe. I even give Mommy a gingerly hug on the way to bed.

"Won't Santa get burned by the fire coming down the chimney?"

"Oh, the embers will be out long before Santa comes!" My mother's eyes roll theatrically.

"But shouldn't Santa have an apple, and are two cookies enough?"

"Remember, he will have something to eat in the living room of each chimney he climbs down!" Mother paints a cornucopia of plenty.

For me, the scrawny little seven-year-old, this is the moment of the year that makes all the others bearable. To be able to communicate with this marvelous Being one never sees, and to know there will be a note in his handwriting, and cookie crumbs waiting in the morning to prove he exists redeems, temporarily, my distrust of things earthbound. Daily living is entangled for me with a mother, usually tense and perspiring, whose very breath and body odor repel me. But at times like this, she is magnificent, all-knowing. Hasn't she, often frightening and wild but at least truthful, promised me that Santa really exists? She has even shown me a "Letter to Virginia" who doubted also, and whose query to some newspaper is answered and printed each year so that all doubting children will know Santa is not a lie. In addition, our mother has embellished the ceremony this particular year by pointing out that if I can just wake up for a moment around midnight, and peer out the window, I might catch a glimpse of the flying magician in his sleigh against the moon, his reindeer bounding gracefully over chimneys. I might hear their hooves prancing on the roof top . . .

"I will wake up!" I vow, dancing up the stairs. On this night even my chilly bed turns to fairyland. I manage to wake up briefly and look out my window on a stillness like a tableau with only a star here and there.

Christmas morning that year was at its peak, the entire living room transformed. The stockings on their cord over the mantel were bulging with protruding boxes and ten-cent store toys spilling out of their sagging tops. There were paper doll cutout books leaning against the chimney bricks and a doll cradle and sleds and a Lionel train for my brothers, and crayons and coloring books. Each of us family members had our own chair stacked with beribboned bundles. There was even a new red Flexible Flyer sled for two propped next to the fireplace with a tag on it "from Santa." And a new Betsy-Wetsy doll, one size up from the last, in its own trunk with a set of baby clothes and a bottle with a nipple.

Reigning over the transformed living room was the short-legged table with Santa's Note, containing letters turned backward in the short message, "Thank you, children, for never forgetting me. Santa."

He had been there! Never mind that I had not managed to see him. He had descended the chimney right into our own living room, secretly. I was in ecstasy. Santa is real and he lives! For me, that was the lifesaver I clung to in our home life. If this woman I mistrusted could materialize a world overnight where joy and love and perfection conquered misery, it wiped out my bafflement, my desperation for a mother who didn't scare me, repel me. That morning I fused Mommy with Santa Claus totally in my desperation for security. I gave my heart to her in total innocence.

Children who have grown out of believing cannot abide others persisting in such fantasy. The following year as Christmas approached a whole classroom of eight-year-olds tried to persuade me that Santa Claus was a fake.

"Julie, Santa Claus is just your parents wrapping all that stuff up!"

"It is not, it is not!" I insisted, my whole being at stake, built upon Mother's word. "My mother promised me he is true. She even showed me a letter from a girl to a newspaper, and the newspaper answered that Santa Claus is real too!"

They shook their heads in scorn. "You're just dumb, Julie. Grow up."

I held them off in a noble struggle. My being was being stoned, brutalized, along with my mother. Our third-grade teacher is present in this sketchy memory, witnessing this scene, bemused, but not inter-vening. My defense was not so much a defense of Santa Claus as it now was becoming a defense of my mother. My mother was not a liar!

When Aurelia Thompson, a classmate who often walked home with me, finally offered the evidence that I could not deny, tenaciousness had to yield.

"You know that doll you got for Christmas," she purred smugly at the foot of our front steps, "well, I saw that doll in your mother's packages as she went up your porch stairs a few weeks ago."

"You saw my new doll? The one with the straw hat and black curls? In my mom's package?" I studied her, stunned.

It was a crippling blow to believing. I mounted those steps cement-like to a world toppled. The greatest sense was of shame. I had just become sullied. Above all, I didn't want my mother to know that I had discovered the truth. It would become my secret wounding. If my believing was so important for Mommy that she had lied to keep me from the truth, then the truth was something she couldn't face either. I didn't want to disillusion her. Protecting my mother, I became false to myself. The world of ideals, of believing, had suddenly deserted me, leaving my heart shriveled.

Our home was in a working-class neighborhood in Highland Park, Michigan, a town like Jonah in the belly of Detroit, the whale of Henry Ford surrounding it. Here, Ford established his first production-line factory in 1914. It turned out "a chassis an hour" by workers paid an irresistible five dollars a day. Suddenly, the Model T Ford became affordable for millions. Our parents purchased our three-story hip-roofed dwelling in 1932 because the Henry Ford Hospital had hired our father, Dr. Philip Howard, for its new pediatric department. Both my parents had left rural Vermont roots to migrate westward. This block of houses on long, thin lots frames the whole of my early world with its urn-like elms arching over our doll buggies and two-wheelers.

My family, with a docile pediatrician at its supposed head and a volatile mother dominating everything routine in our dining room and bedrooms, seemed unaffected by the Great Depression. Our household favored its own personal brand of melancholy. It had spurts of elation that kept everyone off-center. I idolized my father, the perfect adult I could never quite reach. When he occasionally sang me to sleep with songs from his college years, those sounds were like love notes that wafted me sweetly skyward, especially the Irish lullaby *Tura Lura*. If only my father's arms could cradle me like his singing did. If only he weren't in thrall to my mother.

My mother rarely ate all of her dinner, and yet having a successful meal was tantamount to a cum laude for her. She was a Wellesley

College Phi Beta Kappa with no domestic imagination. Sadly, our dinners suffered from a clockwork sameness. Night one, the fresh, hot roast; night two, the cold roast; night three, roast bits in gravy over toast; and night four, hash. Night five would start over. Yet if you asked for her favorite passage from Scott's *The Lady of the Lake* or a Browning poem, Mother could recite at length. She was not original, she was nostalgic. She longed for something embedded in melancholy. Something in poets and their couplets mirrored her own mysterious secret and dedication to place. The small state of Vermont ruled supreme in my mother's loyalties. The Green Mountain contours around Rutland, with her childhood memories, rivaled her attachment to her husband.

My father had all the qualities of a loving mother, never authoritarian, never critical, never capable of punishment. In my eyes, he was long-suffering. He feared our mother's tirades as we siblings did, shrinking from confrontation. I framed my two caretakers as either noble or deceitful, like characters in a Grimms' fairytale. It was beyond Freudian, more mythic than sexual. I longed for a connection with him, but his wife kept us all wound into our separate cocoons.

Because meals symbolized success or failure for my mother, her fixation gave me an opening to wield my tiny power. Nothing was more tedious than sitting at a dining room table staring at a plate of meat and potatoes. Darting around like quicksilver, I spotted traits that could be manipulated. My mother made the cardinal error of reserving time after every meal to coax bites into me. There we were, just the two of us with no competing brothers. I took a perverse delight in holding the trump card. One night, I remember pushing a small ball of cream cheese round and round on one of our transparent butter plates. The smearing cloud-like design delighted me as Mother's patience neared breaking. She lashed out in frustration.

"Julie, oh Ju-lie! I can't stand this any longer! I'm trying so hard to help you eat! You are just sitting there playing!"

She jumped up in anger. I rose in silence, naughty but triumphant. I *knew* Mommy couldn't be trusted. Did I confuse her in my fantasy with the witch plumping up little Gretel and Hansel for tastier morsels? As we got up from the table, I would go to the kitchen where my father often waited for me. He would give me a spoonful of my favorite olive oil.

A rumble reverberates. Could that be—could that mean? The Cerulean Fairy, dozing as entities of infinity do when not on duty, awakens. Yes. The firmament shakes with that old familiar stride—measured, deliberate, ponderous. Cerulea's friend and ally, the Daemon, approaches. The veil of separation will be tested with a new selection.

The two look down through the gossamer veil that Cerulea weaves and reweaves, never ending. The Daemon speaks.

"Do you see her? I think she is my next candidate. Notice how the girl is manipulating her parent. Spunky, idealistic, but headstrong. She's my contestant."

"Oh, children do that." The Fairy isn't interested. "You're choosing too soon. Patience, Daemon, pick on someone your own age."

The Cerulean Fairy chuckles, knowing the Daemon is ageless.

"You'll find your protagonist soon enough."

No wonder the Julie that I was had little interest in meals. I lived in an emotional fantasyland. My mother, morose and choleric every night, was far from the role model I needed. Something shadowy crept into family life as my father returned from the hospital around 6 .p.m.

What cast that shadow had something insalubrious about it, making our sibling nerves jump and smother giggles. How could such a kind Daddy cause Mommy to sniff and whine and shoot piercing barbs at no one in particular? It had to be about something between the two of them. They tucked us into our beds, then retired to their own bed together. What went on in that room must be what made Mommy so unhappy.

Did I intuit this? In Jerry Stahl's razor sharp tale of depression, *Nein, Nein, Nein!*, he comments, observing his children, "They sense everything. They know even if they don't know they do. Like tiny, two-legged nuance detectors."[2]

2. Jerry Stahl, *Nein, Nein, Nein!. One Man's Tale of Depression, Psychic Torment, and a Bus Tour of the Holocaust* (Ashland, OR: Blackstone Publishing, 2023), 142.

5

Signs of Early Aberration, 1940

A strange episode took place within a year of Mother growing weary of feeding her seven-year-old daughter. I think of it as my first true experience, hard to diagnose, of childhood mental illness.

It came about one night before bedtime. It was Mother who precipitated the game change. It surfaced after an especially frustrating struggle of wills at the dining room table over snubbed spoonfuls of hash. I still held her hostage, my pleasure persisting in having her focused upon me, not Jay, who clung and snuggled up to her despite his older brother's scorn, and not George, who dodged her, causing her to fixate upon him, slipping from her control.

I had just gotten out of the bathtub. My mom was rubbing me dry with a big towel. I danced about on my pencil-thin legs in continual motion to the gurgle of the tub draining. A radiator gave out thin heat, warming the towel. Suddenly her voice grew grave. Seeing me naked must have upset her beyond her already distraught bounds. I have no memory of what she said but something about her words had a deadly portent. I have a clear memory of my response. I looked at her fearfully and inquired, "You mean, I might die?"

My mother may have nodded wearily, or at least she hesitated, eyes diverted. This communicated that dying was a possibility. My parent was uncoupling from the nightly scenario so important to my faulty bonding. I may have distrusted her, but I needed her as all children need their mothers. I grasped the fact my mother would no longer play our little "feed me" game protecting me from starvation.

A week passed. It was nighttime. Dinner was finished. There had been carrots for a vegetable. I had just settled into bed with the light turned off. My parents were still walking around outside my bedroom in the hallway. Suddenly, I felt my windpipe block. I sat bolt upright in bed and screamed.

"Help! I'm dying! I can't breathe! Something is stuck in my throat!"

I gasped for breath. Both my parents came running in, frightened themselves. What happened in the next half hour, I do not know. I was in another world. I kept repeating that I couldn't breathe, and that a carrot was stuck in my throat. My father had me open my mouth wide to inspect it for a foreign object, but could find nothing. Perhaps they gave me sharp blows on the back. I didn't know what was happening. I was dying, choking in terror. I gasped, certain that air was not entering my lungs.

Somehow my parents must have calmed me and assured me that I was not choking to death, or they would have rushed me to the hospital that evening. I fell asleep. But the next morning the panic started again. Soon, I had gotten dressed and my parents took me to the Henry Ford Hospital.

In the examining room, another doctor with my father began to run exploratory tubes and mirrors down my throat to see what might be lodged there. They found nothing. My terror was a total mystery to everyone. Perhaps I had swallowed a carrot slice that had burned my throat slightly and caused a swelling. Whatever the original cause had been, I quickly turned into a child who could not be left alone without the symptoms immediately recurring.

"You were right, Daemon, my friend. I see why you chose this young protagonist. She is starting life with unusual difficulty."

The Cerulean Fairy works the shuttle nervously to repair the small tear in the veil. "Already in crisis. I feel sad for her."

"We must watch and see. This child has a will. Remember, the greater the upset the more chance for learning." The Daemon knows all the survival tricks of humans.

The Fairy counters. "The more chance for failing also."

"There is no halfway on the road to the Final Goal."

Cerulea frowns, smoothing out a wrinkle in the gossamer.

Psychosis, or emotional aberration severe enough to interrupt normal functioning, whatever label one gives it, is as old as recorded history. There are accounts of tribal individuals exhibiting sudden altered behavior that causes consternation among their families. Those around them fear mysterious interventions of alien spirits. In the biographies of certain yogis, there are reports of them, as children, losing consciousness or stiffening suddenly like corpses.[3] After a time, the "possessed" ones either emerge from their episodes transformed or they remain caught in their strange world.

Psychosis in children, however, is called by one group of child specialists a conundrum because of the difficulty of clarity. An article published in *Dialogues in Clinical Neuroscience* comments, "The fantasy lives of children . . . and issues of developing cognition all impair diagnostic accuracy."[4] There is agreement that psychosis in children is

3. Isherwood, Christopher. *Ramakrishna and His Disciples*, Kolkata: Advaita Ashrama, 2001. Pgs 31, 35.
4. Courvoisie, Labellarte and Riddle, *Psychosis in Children: Diagnosis and Treatment, Dialogues in Clinical Neuroscience*, Johns Hopkins Medical Institution, June, 2001

a catch-all term for loss of contact with reality that may differ from gross disturbance of thought forms in adults. My memories of the strange episode concur.

Although no one could discover any physical explanation, the panic and choking continued. My parents quickly figured out that the symptoms needed emotional soothing.

They comforted me with a sense of specialness. To this day I credit them for the way they handled this odd fixation. It had an obvious element of my manipulation in it, but an unconscious one that I needed for self-preservation.

Once my father had figured out the problem was psychological, he and my mother concocted child-centered remedies to encourage self-feeding. For several weeks, I could swallow nothing but hot fudge sundaes, which slipped down easily. I went to my third-grade class at Ferris School with a note to the teacher from Dr. Howard. It instructed her that at lunchtime I was to be allowed to walk across the street to Brown's Creamery, the corner dairy store where I sat alone on a high stool at the counter. Feeling princess-like, I licked spoonful after spoonful of delicious chocolate sauce swirling around vanilla ice cream. It came to an end abruptly two weeks later when the waitress behind the counter had had a bellyful of this behavior. She snapped.

"What are you doing here every day eating these sundaes? Why aren't you over at school with the other kids!"

Put in my place, gradually I returned to class. But evening flare-ups required parental presence at all times, with the reassurance that they would not let me die. Interestingly, my mother became very solicitous during this period. Her nightly anxieties subsided for a while.

The after-dinner nightly meal charades between Mother and me faded. I was emerging from something that felt reptilian. The new skin casing was tender. But the days of enjoying the sundaes at Brown's

Creamery and discovering the pleasure of lifting a spoon to my mouth were healing a lot that was shaky in my life. The special note from my parents for school authorities had entitled me to this pleasure. Mommy and Daddy must surely love me!

The little girl with low investment in the tasks required for survival had come up against an either-or challenge. By crying out "I'm dying," I had dramatically thrust myself into a transition that would, with parental support, lead to my taking responsibility for feeding myself.

Interestingly, while reading Carl Jung's autobiography *Memories, Dreams, Reflections* in graduate school later in life, I came across several comments. At one point, when small, Jung had slipped under a railing of a bridge over a gorge. A caretaker caught him in time and Jung reflected that the incident showed an unconscious suicidal wish, a resistance to his family life. Later, during a childhood period disturbing him at night, when his parents showed the first signs of separation, he talked about his choking spells, interpreting them as related to a home atmosphere growing smothering.[5]

5. C. G. Jung, *Memories, Dreams, Reflections*, trans. R. Winston & C. Winston, (New York: Vintage Books, 1965), 9, 18-19.

6

The Blue Pen, 1960

One night at Forest Hospital, maybe at about 2 a.m., a torturous image flooded my savaged psyche. I had a vision of Peter and our children visiting me, their mother, and their father's first love. In this hallucination, I had been transferred to a permanent state ward. I saw myself, bony spine curved forward, peeking up at the visitors with staring eyes as my stringy gray hair partially hid a face where once had sparkled the exuberant Julie. Peter was accompanied by his second wife, now our daughters' stepmother.

"It's your dear mother, girls. Can you give her the gifts you've brought her?" Peter's voice was sad but affectionate.

"I'm scared of that lady." Celeste was hiding behind her father, clinging to his knees.

I was rocking in a chair in the scenario. Saliva trickled down my chin to add itself to the stains on my hospital gown. The three bereft sisters, in the hands of their kind new caretaker, looked upon this hag with puzzled brows.

It was such an unbearable projection that I felt the greatest service I could offer for all of us would be to end my life immediately. I lay awake picturing just how I would do it. It would be easy. The lovely box of

Crane writing paper sat useless on the small, shared shelf right inside our twin room's closet door, a few feet from my bed. It was tugging at me. Peter had given it to me for Christmas, the sheets edged in navy with my name embossed beautifully on half of them, *Julie Howard Parker*. With the pearly blue fountain pen lying on top in the same box, I would thrust its pen point, uncapped and leaking inky fluid, with a powerful stab into my heart.

Yes. That would be the kindest act I could perform for the relief of all of us. I had a plan. I had an implement. I stepped silently, bare-footed, onto the floor. But at that moment my roommate, tossing and turning, gave a sudden snort, half-waking. I decided to consult her for her opinion. I walked over to her bed five feet from mine and shook her a little. She was an aging woman who sat on her messy blankets during the day staring into space, depressed. Her arthritic hands pulled at her blouse buttons, clenching and unclenching, as she undid them only to button them up again.

"I'm planning to kill myself," I whispered to her. "I see no other way out. What do you think?"

My roommate woke up with a start. She began shouting at me.

"For God's sake! If anyone should take their life it should be me! You've got everything to live for! You've got a husband and three young children. Your whole life's ahead of you!

What's the matter with you? God, woman! Snap out of it!"

The roommate's harangue shocked me. It brought just enough perspective to my obsession to abandon an act I will never know how close I was to committing. It is the only time I considered suicide.

The weaving stops. The Fairy trembles.

"Do you see how close your protagonist came to ending it all?"

"Remember, Cerulea, I am never the Cause of harsh times . . . I simply choose the being to focus on. I count on the Will of the protagonist."

"I prefer to emphasize this human being's longing to heal." Cerulea soothes by nature.

"Longing often falters where Will ekes through. Which was in evidence here, in the middle of that night with the blue pen nearby, when our protagonist reached out?"

"Both. Or neither. Perhaps it was random chance."

"Now that is true pessimism. I believe in the Will as master of Longing."

Cerulea said nothing.

From the first week in the hospital, I began chain smoking without any awareness of where my ashes fell. One day I set a poorly extinguished butt on the bed and a patient noticed it smoldering. I was a fire hazard, but the staff paid little attention. Smoking was accepted, perhaps even encouraged in the 1960s.

At times my mind was peopled with dread personages reminiscent of *Dante's Inferno*. Treacherous characters yielding to bestial appetites formed scenes in my subconscious with props—cages, locked doors, iron-barred enclosures. Continually with me was the sense of wandering in a "selva oscura," or dark forest, as Dante described it, from which no being can exit if the filament breaks. Myths tangled in my chaos. I became a Theseus trying to slay the Minotaur, grasping blindly for

Ariadne's golden thread. One night, hallucinating, I was moving through an almost palpable black corridor passing cells inhabited by crazed beings. One maniac in particular came to the bars of her cage, her crooked knuckles reaching for me. With eyes like coals, she stretched a bony finger through the iron.

"Come here, my dear," she wheedled, clawing cunningly, urging me to yield to the pull of her sexuality.

I sensed her nymphomaniac derangement and deadly longing for sexual fulfillment. She was I and not I. Panicking, I hurried on in my sleep. That way led to Hell's eternity. There were deadly characters in other cells, but only she stood out in memory. The nightmares that visited me in bed were indistinguishable from the nightmare I entered upon waking. The axe continued its daily descent.

It didn't matter whether the attack was from within or without. Refugees torn from their familiar lives by war, infantry on the front line stepping over dismembered bodies of buddies or tortured prisoners, all must join a nightmare not too different from the one I was living, a world gone insane. A bewildering Hell cracks the psyche in any of these cases. Emily Dickinson expressed something like it in her poem:

> *Far safer through an Abbey gallop,*
> *The stones achase*
> *Than, moonless, one's own self encounter*
> *In lonesome place.*
> *Ourself, behind ourself concealed,*
> *Should startle most . . .*

Many of us patients were clinging to the thread of "what we were before." Though in my current state I had no capacity to reconnect with my lost psyche, "what I was before" did exist, on that fragile filament. It held, like a downed power line, my love for life, vitality so integral to my being that, even twisted by sick forces, it had sustained a marriage partnership and the birth of three children before giving way.

I had now passed eight weeks sequestered in my inner purgatory at Forest. Two months earlier, Peter and I had been a team, deeply in love, clinging to one another for qualities we each saw in the other. He felt deep affection for the zest and selfless courage of his mother, who had recently died of a heart condition. For her son, I wanted to be like her, one of my many ideal adults. Peter was the earner, acquiring employment skills at a manufacturing company; I was the exuberant homemaker creating family fun. I had bonded almost like an older sister with our three miniature offspring. Peter was a natural nurturer, taking over with the two eldest at dusk the moment he closed the front door behind him. We were a tight little unit. Suddenly, the buckle holding us sashed together had broken. Parallel catastrophes now unfolded, the internal one torturing me, the external one whiplashing Peter into keeping four lives clasped together.

As he lost all but his grip on the steering wheel on that first drive back from the hospital, Peter later told me he had pulled to the side of the road where he broke down, shattered. His collapse of normality was just as severe as mine. He soon had, however, the prop of tasks that must be done to assure the physical and emotional survival of a family bereft of a mother. My vanishing became Peter's mandate.

"You know, after several minutes, bits of a way forward came together a little," he remembered. "I had to face a giant reorganizing task, and sort it into manageable pieces. Our three children became my key focus."

The three sisters would anchor their father as he rearranged his life for them, no matter what happened to their mother. They would give him a reason for living, a mission, even, terrible thought, a memory one day of their institutionalized maternal parent. Two tots waiting for their father would make the return from work brighter, lightening his worry over his hospitalized wife and the financial burden to be borne with the help of her parents and his father. He returned to the home he had grown up in and told little Diane what had happened.

"Mommy is sick in the hospital. We are going to stay here with Grandpa D.D. for a little while."

"Why is she sick?"

Diane, not yet four, looked puzzled, then turned away, worrying perhaps that she herself had caused the trouble. Peter no longer recalls what he told her.

He went back to our York Road house with its as-yet uninhabited additional bedroom and picked up the address book in the kitchen drawer under our phone. My parents, knowing this third pregnancy had been a surprise, had foreseen the possibility of further emotional troubles for their daughter. I had left the army base and returned home to them in Detroit three years earlier on an emergency flight with tiny Diane in my arms. Now, they were planning an exciting trip to Africa to join a missionary pediatrician and his wife in the Belgian Congo. The young doctor, during a residency at the Henry Ford Hospital, had invited them to visit the primitive clinic he operated in the jungles of central Africa. My parents were enthused, but they knew they would be deep in the heart of the Congo at the time I might become symptomatic after giving birth.

Mother made a prescient plan. She wrote to her younger sister, Sophie in New York, to ask her if she would stand by, ready to fly to Chicago should we need her help. She gave Sophie our home phone number, and made sure Peter and I had Aunt Sophie's. I had been doing so well the need seemed unlikely to us as they prepared for the African adventure. Two weeks later they were adjusting to the sounds of drums near the humble infirmary, which was close to a Bambenga pygmy village when the telegram arrived.

Now Peter opened our address book and dialed Aunt Sophie. Petite, shy but with a streak of devilishness that led to little bursts of teasing, she arrived on the plane two days later, silver flask tucked into her purse in case the Parkers were teetotalers. Peter's father, the recent widower, served her a Manhattan and was uplifted by her presence. She added a light touch for a day or two, and then, with two-month-old Celeste in her arms and a baby bag of formula and bottles, she boarded a plane back to Scarsdale, New York. There, the nine-week-old newborn waited for the return of her grandparents from Africa.

Peter began to make trips transferring clothes, toys, storybooks, highchairs and playpens to the roomy house fifteen minutes away on Plainfield Road in a rural part of La Grange, Illinois. Nancy, the Parker's longtime housekeeper, suddenly had not just Mr. Parker senior to cook and clean for, but three additional family members, little Katherine in diapers. Peter combed through the *Chicago Daily News* classifieds for women seeking daytime employment. He interviewed several candidates and settled upon Zenoba, a wiry, efficient 40-year-old who arrived by train Sunday evening and stayed through the week.

As night fell Peter would open his arms to Diane and Katherine running to him as he returned from work. He would shake the carton of Tinker Toys onto the rug before dinner. Then he'd watch Katherine push wooden shapes through Old Mother Shoe with its triangles and square windows. He helped her learn to feed herself Nancy's fine meals. Then he shared the bathing and prepared the two for bedtime after dinner with Zenoba.

And every week he called the hospital.

"How is my wife Julie doing, Dr. Lacroix?"

"I don't see any progress."

Peter rented our home to a family that signed a month-to-month contract.

My parents, deeply worried and supportive, had picked up baby Celeste in Scarsdale twelve harrowing days after Aunt Sophie's return home. They had chartered an emergency flight out of the Congo, landing first in Côte d'Ivoire, then Paris and, finally, in New York at La Guardia Airport. With Celeste now in her fourth pair of arms, they had flown back to Detroit to begin caring for her with the love and expertise of her pediatrician grandfather and my mother's reliability in a crisis. But my parents were devastated; I was their second sibling to succumb to psychosis.

George had had a complete emotional breakdown in graduate school at Union Theological Seminary in New York City. He had spent two years at Austen Riggs Center, a psychiatric hospital in Stockbridge, Massachusetts. The distinguished psychotherapist Erik Erikson was a staff member who accepted George as his patient. Erikson had found George interesting, possessed of a complex that mirrored one of Erikson's own: the overpowering parent that causes separation trauma. Erikson called it the "Medusa Complex." He wrote often about my brother, whom he referred to as the Seminarian. George met a fellow patient, Patricia, in the hospital, married her and the two had a loving, resilient daughter. Later, George switched professions and became a prominent eye surgeon in New York City. He and Patti now sent gifts of cookies and notes of encouragement to me at Forest. They assured me they knew I would heal. Their confidence gave me hope—the crumbs I had longed for from my older brother—now of salient significance.

My family members played admirable, essential roles. But it was Peter's enduring commitment and unfailing nurturing of two of his three children, despite long workdays, that sustained what was left of our family. The warmth and sensitivity of this gentle man had always enhanced his masculinity and attraction in my mind. He had told me about his upbringing on our first date, about his love for his fragile mother, racing against time with a severely damaged heart. She was central to his boyhood security.

Life, it appeared, was repeating itself for Peter. He had delighted in my exuberance and recognized that these qualities, like his mother's, come at a cost. Was he to lose me too, the two female loves of his life?

The Cerulean Fairy asks in a whisper, wings aflutter, "What do you think about this partner, Daemon my ally? He seems vital."

"He will play a role. She has an advocate, but for how long? He will be tested too."

"I am betting on this couple."

"Cerulea, bet away . . . destiny is in their hands, not ours."

"Oh, not entirely. They vaguely sense us, somewhere in their psyche."

7

The Stolen Talisman, 1936-1945

Reaching the corner where California Street met John R Street, a busy thoroughfare we knew we must never go beyond, I stared at her red tricycle, the first I had ever seen.

"Is that yours?"

"Um hmm. What's your name?"

I was five years old. A special child and her family, the Harrises, had moved into a house down the street from ours. Diane was cycling toward me on the sidewalk when I approached her, pushing my doll carriage. I stopped to watch this newcomer as her feet pushed the pedals forward and backward. She was taller than I was and had thick, wiry brunette braids and glasses. Her brown eyes smiled as she asked my name in a voice both soft and mellow. It was instant attraction. Soon Diane and I were inseparable, but of very different natures.

Diane was a tomboy, secretly adoring my brother George. She was more interested in model trains than she was in playing with dolls. My impulsiveness could strike unexpectedly like an adder's tongue. My new friend was calm and gentle but had a knack for maneuvering around my doll absorption to get her way in games. Her cleverness infuriated me. One day in our living room a dispute arose. Diane wheedled.

"If we play marbles first, maybe George will play with us and then leave us alone, and we can play house. Here, I'll set up the box so you can win this time; let me cut the little door wider . . . you can even have the box closer 'cuz I'm bigger than you are."

"I *hate* marbles! It's a boy's game!

Diane recalled that at that point, I seized our India brass letter opener and stabbed her in the knee. I believe her memory. That letter opener on my father's desk had a strange bend in it, used to pry open a stuck drawer. But a knife did exist already in my tiny psyche. We both have vague recollections of me grabbing her by the braids and swinging her left and right. I loved fiercely and raged with equal passion. Diane, in her calm way, forgave me over and over with a loyalty which I returned unwavering. Once spotting me walking to school with Daisy, a classmate, Diane came running up from behind to join us. The girl kicked Diane, then snarled.

"Why does she always have to butt in!"

I was outraged. "That was mean!"

Immediately I turned my back on Daisy and ran to Diane, who had dropped back in pain, eyes moist.

"I'll never walk with Daisy again!" I comforted her.

"You are my best friend." Diane smiled. It was her steadiness I loved, and vulnerability.

Mr. and Mrs. Harris chatted and smiled at us girls when I was invited for a meal, including me in the decision process. I basked in the geniality of this unfamiliar household at the dinner table. But it was Mrs. Harris whom I fell in love with. She became my "ideal mother." I wanted to be at the Harris home every minute; in fact, I wanted a bit of the Harris household in my hands.

One afternoon, when no one was in their living room for a moment, I managed to climb up on a chair in front of Mrs. Harris's walnut secretary. It had glass doors over shelves containing English Toby jugs and knick-knacks. The object of my desire was a small circle of white ceramic angels playing musical instruments. Stealthily, I reached in, removed two of the angels, closed the doors, climbed down from the chair, and rushed home with my trophies without being noticed. Once through the door, out of breath, I told my mother that Mrs. Harris had given me the angels. Mother, puzzled and dubious, called Mrs. Harris.

"Helen, did you give Julie these ceramic angels that she has just brought home?"

Mrs. Harris laughed. "I guess Julie just wanted to borrow those angels for a little while."

My mother returned the angels. I never missed them. My budding kleptomania was nipped, and the success of my stealth must have satisfied the longing.

In many ways, I had flourished in a richly stimulating childhood. I was passionately invested in people who were comforting, in places that coddled my tiny ego and in the engaging activities that my mother encouraged, especially connected to holiday celebrations. No one would have fingered me as headed for mental illness in later adolescence. I was a miniature leader much of the time, full of confidence.

A second bit of fortune descended one day when Aunt Ellen, a widow, came to live with us for two years. She was my father's unconventional older sister. Free-spirited and Bohemian, she had married Uncle Frank, an artist, and ridden off on her honeymoon behind him on an early Harley-Davidson motorcycle. Her wild shock of short gray hair flew around as she played games with us, crawling around on the floor. She had spent time on the island of Barbados where she fell in love with indigenous culture and music. She often hummed spirituals as she helped cook or clean. Mother bonded with her liberalism and early interest in social causes, especially those that addressed poverty and prejudice. Even though Aunt Ellen experienced one tragedy after another, losing first her husband, then her son in an auto accident, losses could not extinguish her buoyancy.

Aunt Ellen's addition to our family of quixotic crosscurrents helped save us from self-destructing. We Howard children now had two maternal forces that dovetailed. When Mother pouted or lashed out, Aunt Ellen would wink at us.

"C'mon kids. Let's go to the living room to play Hide and Seek. It's my turn to seek this time!" Then she would add, "And George, you have to hide with the others. You can't leave us to work on your model airplane." Aunt Ellen was on our side; she knew George never played fair if he wasn't leader. But she joked and won him over.

The only sign that Aunt Ellen felt sadness now and then was when she sang to herself, usually on a Saturday night when our parents were invited out. The words I especially loved were *Sometimes I feel like a motherless child.* I ran to her and threw my arms around her, my heart aching. I would sing along, especially the last lines, *A long way-y from home, from home, a long way-y from home.* Aunt Ellen explained she had learned that spiritual in a Barbados church. When she had to leave us, I was as sad as my father.

"Aunt Ellen," I asked, "Why can't Daddy and I go with you?"

"I'll come again, Julie. Don't you worry." I cried as she headed downtown toward Michigan Central Station to the Wolverine train traveling eastward. She never did come again and died early of cancer.

Imperturbable Aunt Ellen was only second to my love for faithful Diane and my worship of her mother, Mrs. Harris. These two might have been enough to see a quirky little personality through future catastrophes. But a third bit of fortune had an even more exhilarating influence on those early years. When the elementary school year ended, as our teachers were assessing us on sturdy yellow report cards, my mother was packing suitcases. She was preparing for the 700-mile trip east toward the small state of Vermont. Our spirits rose with hers as she pronounced the magic words, "We're going *home!*"

My mother was born in tiny Wallingford surrounded by thriving dairy farms. But we were headed to Rutland, the larger town nearby at the foot of Mt. Pico and Killington where her eye doctor father had moved the family to set up his practice. We would spend the summer in our grandfather's magical gingerbread estate with turrets and stained-glass windows and a moth-eaten stuffed bobcat in the attic. Without my father, who would come later, Mother would start out on the journey driving with us three siblings. As we crossed the state line from New York into Vermont she would pull over by the roadside and stop a moment.

"Oh, smell it children! Can't you smell Vermont already?"

We sniffed the air with her, surrounded by newly mown hayfields. What we inhaled was our mother's transformation. We were entering the "land of our mom." We were headed into idyllic weeks in Vermont where a deep summer safety replaced my fear of a mother bewitched nightly at home. Awaiting us were favorite relatives and gently rolling blue-green mountains that form an ancient ridge dividing the state into slopes that descend into valleys and hollows. We were headed to the communities where our parents had first played together, related by marriage, in the Otter Creek valley dotted with black and white Holstein cows. Sloping eastward, especially farther north, were rocky hill farms that struggled to scratch out existences facing New Hampshire. Judging by our mother, I realized that Vermont never let go of those who had grown up beneath Green Mountain summits. To us children who had not, their embrace extended, instilling in us the feeling we belonged.

Rutland spirited our whole family into another world like Dorothy's Oz wizard, giving us heart, courage, and less scattered brains. It changed George. It changed me. It changed our family dynamics by rearranging alliances of which we were not aware.

In Vermont, Mother was loving, kind, and ideal, like Mrs. Harris. There were *two* mothers in Vermont, because her younger sister, our Aunt Sophie, charming and petite with eyes looking for mischief, arrived in Rutland to crowd into the same home at about the same time for the same two months with her three daughters. Agnes, the eldest, was a year younger than I, but less airy, knowing directional north from south and how to tell time. In school I had failed over and over to grasp the import of two clock hands circling each other, slicing in to my dream world.

I feared Agnes would reveal my ignorance to my great aunt, whose instructions to us upon arriving were for me to take my suitcase up to the south bedroom, and for Agnes to take hers to the north one. She did so, giggling at my confusion.

I loved Agnes as I loved Diane. Our mothers played house through their offspring like old times, enjoying an unusual bond with their solitary father. They relived memories of visits to elderly aunts and uncles by arranging overnight stays for us. We children created generational continuity.

There was, however, something darker about the euphoria we dwelled in. This same Vermont childhood concealed a secret for my mother and perhaps her sister. It held the key to the origin of Mother's nightly depression back in Michigan. Only toward the end of Mother's life would unsavory truths emerge. The bliss bewitching us in Vermont was linked to that hidden darkness.

These two sisters rushed compulsively back to their Rutland childhood scenario minus husbands. Had the hills of Vermont truly claimed their hearts or was it to comfort their father, the doctor who had lost his wife, Mary, the year I was born? If the latter, why did Mother and Aunt Sophie never mention her, their mother, my recently deceased grandmother, whose Haviland china we ate off, whose birds-eye maple table we sat at, whose iron beds we slept in? Her ghost must have hovered everywhere in the high-ceilinged rooms for her two adult daughters. Yet there was never mention of their mother, no effort ever made to picture her for us, anchoring her memory in us. Instead, the glee and chatter of us six cousins racing up and down the brown creaking stairway expunged this mysterious grandparent. If there was something sorrowful or sordid being masked over, we did not feel it.

Missing from this summer stage were two dramatis personae: our fathers. Though I longed to have my father in Vermont, he would show up for a week or two and depart, his work drawing him back to the familiar hospital corridors where patients waited their turn to see Dr. Howard. Only as an adult have I realized his true love was the Henry Ford Hospital. He had left New England behind for a fulfilling career in medicine. The Ford doctors were his companions. He played tennis and squash with "Johnny" Johnston, head of the pediatric department, and Dave Davidson on the hospital courts. They were on call for one another, a team often facing fatal illnesses in small patients. These summers free from his wife's nightly frenzies and children were surely Heaven on Earth for him, never long enough.

8

Rays of Hope, 1960

"Oh, I'm so scared. I don't know what to do. I'm so scared, so scared!" It was Muriel. After eight weeks at Forest, the muscles in my neck could lift my head again and I began to notice other patients. Most of us were frozen in nightmares that blurred the distinction between daytime and sleep. We were paralyzed with the thought that we'd never get well. Muriel rubbed her thumb, index and middle finger together, pacing back and forth with a cigarette in her other hand, repeating the phrase over and over. She grew especially agitated in the dining hall and made me shudder because I feared my symptoms mirrored hers. We both smoked.

A sign that one wouldn't or couldn't recover was the rumor, running through hospital corridors from patient to patient, that someone was being "transferred." A simple comment, "Have you heard? Muriel is being taken to Metropolitan," sent chills through each of us. We patients knew that Metropolitan was the low-cost state institution reserved for the most resistant cases, a permanent sentence. Metropolitan meant madness with no way out, the repository of zombies.

Forest Hospital had nurses supervising medications and psychiatrists who came and went daily during my stay. Volunteers brought fresh flowers, and aides took us on walks or supervised our digging in a small spring garden inside the fence barrier. One German woman watered window plants weekly and always smiled at me.

"Do you think I'll ever get well?" I asked, clinging to her pleasant face.

"You will come over this," she answered. Her twisted word order made her message stick with me. Loving language, I repeated her phrase in my mind like a mantra.

There was a "security" cell that may have had padding. Attendants were always on-site, trained to restrain patients having episodes harmful to themselves or others. We often simply sat silent in the lounge or our rooms, bombarded from within. At times we'd hear screams coming from that cubicle.

An occupational therapy room had a kiln, a sewing machine, clay and painting materials to provide activity. My first creation—an object rich with symbolism—was a coiled clay ashtray for Peter with delicate tomahawks circling its edges. A psychotherapist would have plumbed that imagery with an outpatient, but our minds were too disturbed for cognitive processes. We were like ghosts on a game board, tokens stuck on a square or moved backward and forward by hands shaking dice in some alien reality.

After three months at the institution, I was the longest-staying inmate there. Patients came and went. I remained. One woman arrived psychotic. She didn't know where she was or why she was in the hospital. In two weeks she "snapped out of it" and was discharged. There was no predictable pattern to patient suffering. Some were in constant states of torture, like Muriel, visibly deteriorating before our eyes.

But I began to feel, a sliver at a time, better. It was a small sensation of emergence at first, rapidly erased by renewed fears.

"Arletha, help me! Do you think I will ever get well?"

"Of course you will, Julie."

Getting well was the dream that never let me go.

The nurses spent most of their time behind a glass-walled cubicle with typewriters, phones and patient records. They either were cheery as they looked out at us in the lounge, or scowling. I befriended Arletha. Repeatedly, after an especially frightening episode, I would run to the glass enclosure seeking her.

My natural gregariousness and attraction to others—to those with warm smiles or racial diversity or even a certain eccentric marginality—began to resurface. The brawny attendants were trained to react immediately to de-escalate problems. They calmed patients down and put them temporarily in the security room. One day, feeling I was about to explode, I ran to the one I had befriended and begged him to take me to that cell.

"Tie me up, Amahl. I'm about to blow apart."

He smiled. "You? Naw . . ."

I insisted. He walked me to "security," leaving the door open, and sat on the chair next to a hard cot talking to me until the pressure dissipated.

"Julie, you gonna be fine. Just take your time. You gotta be patient."

"Amahl, that seems like a dream. I can't believe it will ever happen. Not for me."

Most of us at Forest longed for signs of healing. The slightest improvement or stride forward became, "I'm almost cured!" Then, symptoms would return with a vengeance. It was not unlike what prisoners go through when a possible discharge is dangled before them, then rescinded. Our minds were our imprisoners. In a card George wrote to me, he suggested a dictum that he had found valuable.

"Julie, it is 'three steps forward, two steps backward.' Just hang in there."

George's input meant more to me than any other person's. And the saying was correct. Great leaps of euphoria now accompanied each palpable sign I felt of emerging from the inferno. Then would come the two steps backward, almost unbearable, like a satanic jokester's trifling.

Healing, the goal I so desperately longed for, now shimmered like a desert mirage. A kind of see-saw effect set in. Each small sense of progress triggered a cunning retort from my sick psyche.

"You are trapped . . . that way out is blocked too . . . give it up." A demonic little fiend would float on my mind's screen, a sort of tongue-lashing dragon with seahorse shape, breathing out mockery. Wave after wave of mental nausea drowned my feeble efforts to connect new neurons. But time was an ally.

"Daemon, our protagonist is entering the risky back-and-forth period between hope and despair. I cannot sit by without speaking up!"

"Cerulea, you know that there is little we can do but observe. Remaining steadfast, never deserting is our role. This protagonist longs to overcome suffering. Setbacks are part of the way to the Final Goal. What other way is there?"

"Through joy, through lightness, through tears of gratitude!"

The Daemon, seeing Cerulea's iridescent wings try to rise rather than sag, glances away.

"Memory of those fades even faster than memory of pain, Cerulea. Setbacks slowly wear protagonists down to a state of malleability."

"Or state of a zombie. I care about this protagonist!"

"You intimate I do not? My eternal partner, you know me better than that."

One day, I realized I would never know what my youngest daughter looked like in her first months. Curiosity about this infant I had lost along with my sanity was a first sign of recognition that a family waited for me beyond Forest walls. The sudden interest in Celeste also led to a slight resumption of verbal skills. Using the fateful blue pen and vellum paper for the first time, I wrote a note to my parents.

Dear Mom and Dad, I am feeling better. Could you please have a picture taken of Celeste so I will know what she looks like?

They did so promptly, taking her to a photography studio. I received a silver-framed black and white print of her head and shoulders, three different views. She was about five months old in the photograph, smiling, cutting her first teeth, a beautiful little face looking left, right and center in a sweater Mrs. Harris had knit for her. I recognized its raglan sleeves like those she had sent to me earlier for Diane and Katherine. I treasure that picture today. It is the only formal trace of a baby I had given birth to torn from her mother's arms at a moment when her first earthly security was the warmth of skin and breast, and the sound of a voice soothing her whimpers.

At this juncture, after about three months had elapsed, I decided in a three-steps-forward moment that I was ready to return home. My histrionic teen-aged roommate and I were playing daily games of bumper pool. She had shared with me her interrupted plan to commit double suicide with her boyfriend, staging her own little Romeo and Juliet.

"Dr. Lacroix, I am ready to be discharged."

"No, you are not."

I rebelled. "Why can't I leave this place? I've been a good patient."

"Because I don't think you are realistic," the doctor replied. Then he left.

Realistic? I puzzled over its meaning. How does one become realistic? To this day, I still think I am not very "realistic" if it means seeing life as tedium and drudgery. No doubt he was waiting for me to show awareness of our tiny daughters minus their mother, or worry over how I was failing them.

The descending-axe episodes were growing less frequent. Peter was finally allowed to visit me. The closeness of sitting next to him on the bed in my room stirred up distorted sexual feelings that reminded me of that hallucination of the caged nymphomaniac. I could sense the warning wave of nausea threatening my fragile cohesion.

"Move a little farther away, Peter."

"Why? I am so longing to hold you, to be with you again!"

I couldn't tell this loving man his closeness endangered me. Otherwise, the visit went quite well. Shortly afterward I was permitted to go out for a meal with Peter. Two weeks later, I was discharged.

9

In Between, 1940-1951

"C'mon you guys. Girls are sissies. Horrible. Crybabies." George, age eleven, tried to persuade his buddies to sign up for his Hate Your Sister club. Although few enrolled, the club was a daily reminder that my brother scorned my existence. To seek his respect I played tough. In nightly games it was my younger brother Jay who would cry, hit by a hard-soled moccasin in George's favorite game of Slipper Fight. Jay was my foil, waving a flag of surrender so I wouldn't have to.

George had been Mother's joy and fulfillment from birth. She adored babies; having an infant was like playing with dolls again. And a son! There hadn't been a son in the family for a generation. Babies were easy, needy, depending totally upon their mothers, gratuitously empowering them.

At about age two, just as George's small will began to assert itself, I arrived. Will o' the wisp Julie attracted attention. Two-year-old George was dethroned by a newcomer. He turned hostile.

Jay, three years my junior, looked up to his older sister. He was a sunny sidekick. He was Mother's first child who was truly cuddly and affectionate. He would climb into her comforting lap without fearing inundation. She adored this third child. She could stroke him and smother him to her heart's content, even nuzzling his little pop-up penis as an infant. That image of her head bending forward toward what my body lacked etched itself into memory. The picture was buried deeply, perhaps knifelike. Bound up with it was a shame and dismissal of my female gender.

Caught between an older contemptuous sibling and a younger brother glued to my mother, I sealed myself in a brittle shell. I would never show weakness that might diminish me in George's eyes. I armed myself so tightly and sharply that my weapon's edge sliced me at times and those I loved at others.

But lodged in another part of me was a magnet drawn toward gentleness, kindness, vulnerability. It tugged me toward my father, to Aunt Ellen's singing, to Diane, and to her mother, my beloved Mrs. Harris. And to stories that righted wrongs. My mother read me stories.

The first magical book she shared with me was Marguerite De Angeli's *Skippack School*. I slept with it under my pillow. Its protagonist was Eli, a mischievous boy like George. My favorite picture was of naughty Eli in his Pennsylvania Dutch britches being gripped by his father and taken out to the woodshed for a whipping. Might I have seen in that resolute eighteenth-century parent the protector I needed with the strength my father lacked? A dreamlike spell cast by her reading and my listening joined Mother and me, perhaps both longing for male assertiveness. Eli repents, becoming loving and thoughtful. Could George repent like Eli? It was my secret longing.

George did begin to change just before the onset of adolescence. In manual arts class he made me a doll-sized, mahogany-stained cupboard out of pine for Christmas with three open shelves for my Blue Willow tea set. I was in love with it. In Rutland summers, he forgot about his sister-hating club. He rode to the clinic in the downtown Gryphon Building with his oculist grandfather to observe him trying corrective lenses on patients. He had a new feeling of importance playing "doctor's helper." Mother's metamorphosis in Vermont tamed George. It was as if the male role my grandfather played pacified her in contrast to the irritant her husband represented upon each nightly return. In Detroit, my father, drained after a day with patients, mustered his last bit of strength to face his wife's attacks. He had no energy to bond with his sons. The mix of my parents' characters in those early years curdled rather than blended into family harmony.

The Vermont summers prepared the way for a stretch of growing self-confidence as we entered an in-between time. Mother loved these years with us. A new world beckoned to us as Diane and I discovered our budding independence together. We sped through the crunching leaves on our bikes with the wind in our faces. Today that childhood home on California Street is a burned-out hulk in a derelict Highland Park neighborhood, but in the 1940s we roamed our land like the Apache before the interloping white man.

Our lives swelled in that period with a sense of never-ending time. Life *was* time and we were left alone to spend it as we chose. We created our own Oz where parents were behind curtains for a while. Side by side we learned to swim in the grade school pool, sew at the home arts Singer machines and cook an omelet in sixth-grade cooking class. We had a store of free afternoons to fritter away as we wished. There was no cell phone, no "social media," no organized Little League. We read Nancy Drew mysteries, played ball in our backyards and collected foreign stamps. Simply being alive, we inspired each other's ingenuity and learned what friendship entailed, earning Scout badges together. It was like being dipped in a beautiful tincture that could never fade entirely. And there was camp.

Camp Hanoum was my first truly non-ordinary experience in the hills of Thetford, Vermont. A circle of our voices in unison would sing *Rise, Oh Spirit!* to the curling smoke of a pungent outdoor fire as evening settled over our hillside tent sites. We would lie in cots watching shooting stars while melody floated down from our music counselors practicing Mozart in the gabled hall perched on the slope above our tent rows. Camp life shepherded me and Diane, the steady sidekick who countered my impulsiveness in the same ways Peter would later, into early adolescence. We swam and hiked and rode horseback into that heady sub-teen world where crushes are shared in whispers with our tent-mates at night. I swooned over stern and elusive Bidge, the riding counselor barking at me, "Heels down!" in the ring. She had noticed me! The next year it was the director's son, hired in the kitchen. My eyes would seek his in a secret glimpse and smiles "only for each other" as he handed out bowls of chocolate pudding at suppertime.

Whatever damage had been done earlier in my most impressionable childhood years was dormant. It was waiting like a temblor for the forces to build, giving warning quakes during a freshman year at college.

As the final weeks of my public high school senior year drew to a close, I felt at the height of confidence. I had been president of our intercultural club and had led a youth group at church where love budded into kissing and hugging my first boyfriend. Most classmates were making a safe little jump to the University of Michigan. Proudly taking more risk, I was leaving home for a horizon 700 miles distant, Middlebury College.

Once on Middlebury's campus, however, I crumpled. An unknown Julie was quivering inside the knight in cardboard armor. I had mistaken Vermont as my second "home," composed of memories of welcoming aunts and the mountain contours surrounding them. Middlebury was not the Vermont I knew. Most of the students were from East-Coast preparatory schools. They found me quaint and tease-worthy.

"Say 'spider' for us, Julie. Where did you say you're from?"

"Detroit. It's in Michigan. Your family car was probably made there."

I burned inside. My thriving city was to them a backwater town off the map of New England. Their laughter hurt. But prep school had taught them how to take notes in class lectures. For the first time, I worried about failing academically. I ended that freshman year shaken.

With no safety behind or before me, I returned to sophomore classes at Middlebury in misery. Mother saw me off with a long, sad embrace; I clung to her, tears welling. Mysterious forces were at work throughout this first family separation. I shrank into isolation. I had made no friend who would be waiting on campus for my return that second year. No roommate, academic class, field or professor had ignited my passion. I appeared to be heading for perilous shoals.

What transpired instead was inexplicable by the laws of either developmental or abnormal psychology. A sudden change came over me, erasing all loneliness and defeatism that had ended my first year at Middlebury. It was as if a guiding spirit sensed something life-altering was about to take place, needing me to be ready, receptive, even radiant. A joyfulness came over me for no reason and nothing could erase it. Applying for a role on the college newspaper, I hardly saddened upon being rejected. Auditioning as an alto for the college's famous choir, I was sure of acceptance since I had sung in glee clubs all through high school. But it bothered me only momentarily to be turned down. What was erasing my disappointments? What was about to happen?

"*Every protagonist you choose, Daemon, alters my weaving.*"

"*That is what holds our interest in humanity, Cerulea.*"

"*What caused her to change so suddenly from dejection to buoyancy?*"

"*Destiny, Cerulea. Destiny plays by its own rules. It senses what is needed for next steps.*"

"*I suppose you would say we control neither Destiny nor human beings.*"

"*True, my Winged Friend. We only observe. But we are affected by these earthly characters.*"

"*How so?*"

"*We evolve with them. Our Universe evolves, Cerulea.*"

"*Oh, that's too much. Evolving is beyond me right now.*"

10

Limbo, 1960

"Peter, I am scared. It feels like there's no place for me any more in your father's home. I've been gone for too long. No one recognizes me anymore. I hardly recognize myself."

"Just take your time. You've been through a tough ordeal and you are healing. I am so happy to have you nearby. It will be different when we get back into our own house."

He came over to the armchair I had shrunk into, half hidden by its winged back, and took my hand, smiling.

"But that is what worries me the most! What if I fail? What if I can't do my job?"

Peter was probably concerned too, seeing me withdrawn, creeping about on the edges of the hum of daily life. He never let on.

"You are going to be fine. I know you better than you do. Dr. Lacroix wouldn't have discharged you if he hadn't seen your progress. Waiting and worrying with nothing to do is harder than being given responsibility."

Peter's words comforted me.

Dr. Lacroix had discharged me at the end of the fifth month, in mid-June, a month later than I had felt ready. His wise timing avoided the event I most feared: readmission to an institution, "incurable." Peter had come into the lounge to pick me up, causing interest among my fellow patients. They grouped around gaping, longing for glimpses of someone from the outside world. I trembled like any newly released prisoner. An hour later, the walk through the door into my father-in-law's living room of that normal world had felt surreal.

Far from the mother I had been before giving birth to Celeste, I had no feelings for either little daughter. I watched them play with their Lincoln Logs, two small strangers for whom I was a visitor they hardly looked at. Little Celeste in remote Detroit occupied no place at all in my thoughts. But I had withstood and prevailed under the watching Eye. That is all one can do in a psychiatric hospital. My slight re-entry into the outermost periphery of "normal" was still far from a functioning mother's normal.

Peter's retired father, Nancy, his housekeeper, Zenoba, the weekday nanny, and Peter himself, departing in the morning and returning at dinner time, had all created a choreography that left no role for an extra. Peter had provided both paternal and maternal needs to our children for so long they now ran to him at dusk and looked forward to game and book time.

"Hi, Daddy," Diane would greet him, echoing the very words I had used to welcome my own father at 142 California Street. Katherine toddled after her. I observed this, feeling like an extra thumb in the routine. The family renting our house on York Road was in no hurry to move out.

An extended limbo settled upon that summer, full of the kind of pitfalls that face an ex-con discharged to life outside. The axe continued to descend, if not daily, perhaps every other day. My response was the same in the Parker living room as it had been at Forest Hospital. I clutched my head in terror and ran across the rug to the other wall, panting wildly. This amused Nancy and Zenoba no end.

"What's the matter, Julie?" They eyed each other slyly.

I could not respond, but began to resent them both. Trapped in that Parker sanctuary, I noticed my hair graying.

In Detroit, my parents were growing exhausted. They had tended little Celeste for eight months, perhaps imagining that I was now malingering. Their worry over George, their first-born, their brilliant son struck down in graduate school with mental illness, had always taken precedence over the fate of their two other children.

"Julie, I want you to come over and get Celeste as soon as possible. Your mother is growing very tired."

"Oh! Well . . . I don't know. But I'll come. I'll try my best."

My father spoke more assertively than was his custom.

"Your mother and I cannot be rearing your third child indefinitely."

Dutifully, I got on a plane and flew to Detroit. When I arrived at the Tudor house of my parents, I lost what little gain I was making at the Parker home. Approaching the baby threatened my slowly healing psyche. She was a delicate little being in a quiet world of her own with silvery wisps of hair. The tiny stranger's fragility traumatized me. Simply being near her brought back a slight reversal toward early hospital symptoms; nausea followed. Hanging my head at the dinner table, I could neither eat nor talk. It was obvious to my parents that I was not ready to take Celeste home with me. I got back on the plane alone a day later and flew back to Chicago where Peter met me at the airport.

In an appointment with Dr. Lacroix I asked, "Do you think I will ever be able to take care of all three of my children?"

His answer was predictable. "I don't know."

After two months of my foreboding and languishing at the Parker residence, the renters vacated our York Road home. At last I had a role in sight and a mission. The change was miraculous.

"Peter, I think I am going to be okay!" I skipped lightly up and down the familiar porch stairs carrying boxes. My own home, at last! It was the job I needed to recover fully.

"I knew you'd be fine. And I'll get to work on the lawn. The renters did the minimum. Careful! That porch railing is coming loose."

Peter showed not a twinge of apprehension. He was the reliable man I loved and, to be truthful, at times fed upon.

We made trips back and forth reinstalling our furniture. Diane and Katherine raced up and down the stairs, from the room in the new addition to their old bedroom, laughing and hiding and banging closet doors. I scrubbed the stove coated with bacon grease. Something beautiful was extinguishing those qualms at the Parker home: being reliable, being head of a household. My natural buoyancy was returning. I was home, picking up again that bubbly, high-spirited adult role that had deserted and imperiled me. Proving myself to myself was all-absorbing; I felt the prize, wellness, taking form at last.

"How did your day go?" Peter would ask, prepared for a setback perhaps, returning from work.

"Everything is great. I'm feeling stronger and stronger. I walked into town today with the girls and the buggy with its seat down. We bought popcorn and did a little grocery shopping."

Peter smiled and held me in a prolonged hug. I could feel his inner relief, gripping me a little tighter than usual, his palms then circling on my lower back in a massage. His hands were oversized and reassuring, fit for hard work. I felt little waves of actual happiness. My native competence, that outgoing girl on a bicycle, collecting stamps and Scout badges and advancing to Schubert on the piano, was responding to this test of re-entry into functional life. The transition period of marking time, so demoralizing at Peter's father's home, had perhaps been a needed blessing, avoiding a hospital return.

We bought a set of maple bunk beds for the new addition downstairs, and I soon had yards of cotton for curtains and matching bedspreads running through my Singer. Peter installed an intercom so we could hear the girls playing or waking up at night. We hadn't actually moved them into that room yet; they were still in the bedroom across the hall from us upstairs. That added wing had symbolized disturbance from the beginning. It was tied to anxiety and a third child, our tiny Celeste.

The worst of the symptoms faded, along with the descending axe. Wellness seemed within reach. Once again, my parents, hearing how well we all were doing, asked me to come claim Celeste. Mother was growing frantic with insomnia. I tried and failed a second time, flying home with no baby in my arms, fearing I would never be more than a half-mother. Peter was wonderful.

"Just wait ... don't worry about your parents." He had never embraced my mother and father wholeheartedly.

It was now mid-October. Our incompleteness hung over my head, but my job was to prove I could function with the two small sisters we were enjoying. They were ours, we were a family again. Back to my airy style of motherhood, nurturing emotional needs but forgetting our daughters' physical whereabouts at times, I greeted my husband one evening.

"Guess what, Peter. I'm planning to take the girls to the zoo tomorrow!"

Peter hesitated. "The zoo? That's quite a drive, Julie. Ogden Avenue, then to 31st Street. How about waiting until Saturday and we'll go together?"

I wanted to go right away. "Peter, it will be fun for the girls and me. Remember, I'm a Detroiter. I've been driving since I was fifteen."

Peter rarely thwarted my enthusiasm. "Well, be sure to leave and return before traffic gets heavy. You know Ogden at rush hour."

Off we went the next day. I strode ahead among the crowds, stopping at this cage and that, the little girls running along behind me. Suddenly, as I became absorbed in watching a lion roaring, agitated as a press of onlookers gathered, I heard a voice over the loudspeaker.

"We have a little two-year-old here named Katherine who is crying. Please come to the Information Center to pick up your child."

I was chagrined. I took Diane by the hand and the two of us wove through the crowds as fast as we could. I scooped up little Katherine before the shaming eyes of the zoo personnel.

"You got a little carried away, I guess, *Mother*."

Embarrassed, I held little Katherine until her tears abated. When Peter came home that evening, Diane reported the incident excitedly. Peter just looked at me, shaking his head. "Live and learn, my dearest. Live and learn."

II

Recovery, 1960-1963

"I think it would be fun to go to Detroit and bring baby Celeste back with us. Just for the holidays."

Surprised, Peter asked, "Do you think you can handle it with Christmas coming?"

"I'd like to have her with us. It will be a trial. At a happy time."

Healed! The modifier I so longed for was truly shedding its grace upon our family. I had stopped smoking. When I began singing the girls to sleep once more, as my father had for me, all symptoms faded.

I had now been out of the hospital for a summer and a fall. Halloween had grinned in on a seamstress making costumes for her two-year-old and four-year-old with the same excitement Mother had instilled in me, George and Jay for holidays. Diane and Katherine trotted up a street by my side at dusk with a hollow plastic trick-or-treat pumpkin. Two weeks before Christmas, as we were decorating our windowsills with balsam boughs and red candles, the pleasant thought had descended into the festive preparations. It would be lovely to have all three sisters with us for the holiday.

We called my parents to announce I was coming to collect our baby. The very next day. In those days one could buy a ticket and be assigned a seat right away on a plane.

"Oh, dear! We're not ready, nothing is organized or packed," Mother protested. "The timing isn't right at all."

My father cut in and spoke over Mother's hesitation.

"You come right along. Tomorrow will be fine. We'll have everything ready for you."

For the third time, I boarded the plane for Detroit. Celeste was thirteen months old, walking, and I remember her in a spotless gray-green snowsuit with white embroidered hearts circling the collar and hood. Her fine strands of silky blond hair now invited my fingers to touch them, stroke them. She smiled and let me hold her. I did not sense much attachment between her and her grandparents, nor much animation. She had been passed between caregivers too many times. Within twenty-four hours, she and I were on a plane becoming acquainted while a suitcase full of her wardrobe was in the checked baggage.

Christmas that year was a gift for me, and for all of us. Near the glowing warmth of our own crackling flames in the fireplace, I read *A Visit to Saint Nicholas* to the girls, prepared with a roundabout explanation that the 'spirit of Santa is real' if they should ask. Peter held little Celeste on his lap, jiggling his knees as he half sang, half hummed, his own version of Jingle Bells to her. She looked at him, at all of us with searching, confused eyes. Our task would be to make a warm place for her in our family.

We hung beautiful red, green and white angora yarn-for-Santa's beard stockings knit by Mother on a cord over the fireplace, and heaped an abundance of gifts all around the fragrant balsam tree. The next morning, as Diane and Katherine rushed down to the magical bounty, I watched tiny Celeste in her baby chair look out at us solemnly, bewildered by the sudden excitement of sisters trying to pull her into the activity. She did not know us and we did not know her yet. The way ahead for our third child would not be an easy one. I would try to make up for what had happened that could not be helped.

"Aren't you proud of our protagonist, my Daemon friend? She has made it through."

The Daemon notes the veil of gossamer, spread without a wrinkle.

"Correction. She has made it through a major test. She is nowhere near approaching the Final Goal . . . "

"Oh, dear. I thought perhaps . . . "

"Here . . . I know you don't savor my poems, but they are, shall we say, predictive . . . "

"Which poem is it this time?" The Cerulean Fairy twitches slightly. The Daemon recites.

She feels no longer vulnerable. Her healing will endure.

The Cosmos knows quite otherwise, its wisdom crystal pure.

It deals in higher struggle that can seal a human's fate;

It operates upon a plane few ever penetrate.

The threads of my broken mind were reweaving over a gash that would never give way to the same extent again. All that I thought had burned with my incinerated brain cells—the ability to feel affection for Peter and the children, to speak French, to read, write and reflect upon cultural differences, and to laugh again in high spirits—rose from the embers. The demands of motherhood helped recovery.

I bubbled again, with a slight manic tinge. My natural buoyancy would lead to increasingly ambitious projects. Being "well," having triumphed over my beast in the arena, was heady. For now, I enjoyed the playfulness of being mother, home maker, unbridled creator of our daily adventures. In a few years, a new stage, with children in school, would allow time to review the hospital catastrophe from a distance. My search would begin, haphazard and unfocused at first, for why such a horror had happened to me. Interestingly, the determination to understand the causes of my psychosis would lead first into a highly exhilarating project of the type that triggers relapse.

We were happy together. Peter and I enjoyed our basic roles at home, his in work gloves with a shovel, pliers or hammer, mine at my sewing machine creating curtains and matching outfits for our tots. I loved the way he came home at night and modeled responsible fatherhood.

"C'mon, chicks. Let's read a story while Mommy prepares dinner. Shall we pick up the blocks first? Oh, there's a red one under that chair by the fireplace."

He wasn't afraid to put on an apron and chop celery for a Waldorf salad, or show Diane how to set the table. We were a team that functioned. I loved him standing beside me in the kitchen, a sudden hug, a piece of apple popped into his mouth, approving the menu. His unbendable ethics often frowned on, then excused my thoughtlessness, the tricycle in the driveway blocking him from pulling the car in off York Road. As he reported the news, his ability to synthesize events into a comprehensive worldview awed me. I giggled at his bits of gossip from the boys at the office.

"Norm's at it again, calling our new receptionist 'cold as a witch's tits.'"

Norm was the one who complained his wife thought he was lucky to "get it" once a month. Peter may have chuckled, but he was silently circumspect about our own private lives.

A pattern began to assert itself. Peter paid the bills, rotated the car tires, repaired leaky faucets, added decorative railings to our porch. He was safety-minded, as dependable as the earth we walked upon. I began to soar as the children reached school age. My mate often slipped from my awareness as a flow of ideas branched into ever-varying adventures, even decisions made without consulting him.

I thrived on languages, interesting people, foreign cultures, exotic lands.

Flashing from one thought and place to the next, I often collided with my husband.

"Watch out, Julie! My god, if you want me to find that outlet for your lamp, step back! Here, hand me the plug. I'm sorry, Sweetie, but think before you jump."

Peter enjoyed the exuberance in our family, but submerged his preference for quiet companionship and hiking in solitude. He longed for mountains, remoteness from humanity. For now, self-denial worked for him. It worked for him in all but one place. That place was where marriages can succeed or fail. That place was our bedroom.

Night after night, when our three little daughters were finally asleep, the man I claimed to love looked forward to what I dreaded: sexual intimacy. Playing a support role during the day, he now rose to the center of our drama so we could perform, body pressed against body, together. We were a mismatch. My loving man, so grounded and giving, starred and radiated with potency as I froze in misery. I hoped, I tried, I wanted to respond to him, to show my deep affection for him, to enjoy his body entering mine as an act of supreme surrender. I could not. Despite his patient stroking, his soothing coaxing, his ability to hold back and do all in his power to arouse me, I felt nothing. I was as though paralyzed from my navel to my knees. And after Peter, unable to wait any longer, clutched me in an explosion of ecstasy, I sat on the edge of our bed and wept. Something was not healed. I was alive only from the waist up, half blocked to the one whose giving spirit I longed to reciprocate.

"It's all right, my dearest. Don't worry about it. I know you love me." Peter would come around the end of our double bed to sit at my side and offer solace.

I would not be comforted. I did not want to be half a person. Why could I feel nothing? When had this numbness begun? It didn't follow logically the euphoria that had flooded me in Peter's presence in the early stages of our romance. It had been interrupted by my boarding that ship for France. France must be the culprit. But . . . wasn't there a sudden tightening in my response to my growing intimacy with this man before I thought of a student year abroad? Something bizarre in my imagery of him? I continued weeping, night after night. I had recovered, but I was not healed. An enemy hid inside me, tightly barricaded, too humiliating and embarrassing to share with anyone. I needed to find its source.

PART TWO
Middlebury and France
1952-1958

Predating Part One, five chapters show a beautiful love story curdled.
Powerful longings fulfilled in innocence are torn apart by fate. A stranger
appears speaking French.

12

Remembering

"Mama, Daddy has a present for you. Come see."
In our cozy York Road home in early December, I was in the kitchen roasting a special capon inspired by the coming holiday. Diane and Katherine heard the dependable nightly steps of their father on the porch and rushed to the front door to greet him, letting in a blast of wintry air. With three-year-old Celeste following, they burst into the kitchen.

I walked into the living room and there was Peter with a box of twelve beautiful red roses in his arms. Diane, Katherine and Celeste each held a pink rosebud with a ribbon tied around it.

"Do you know what is special about this year, my dearest?"

"I can't think. Tell me."

"Ten years ago at just about this time, you and I met on a ride home from Middlebury to Chicago. It was the greatest thing that ever happened in my life."

"Oh, my darling! No! It was the greatest thing that ever happened in *my* life. We wouldn't be here today with our three daughters if it weren't for that meeting!" The girls watched their parents lock in a long embrace.

After dinner, and after the children had been read stories, sung to and brought glasses of water for the nth time, Peter and I put on an Irving Berlin record in the living room. We began to dance to *Blue Skies, How Deep is the Ocean* and *Always*. At the latter's famous lyrics, I began to cry. Peter tipped my chin upward with his index finger. We looked into each other's eyes.

"How could Irving Berlin get it so right, and with words so simple? Peter, you'll never know how much I love you."

I was streaming tears of happiness for our current joy, and of sadness for the tragedy that had overwhelmed us so early in our life together. Later lying in bed arm in arm, we retold the details of our meeting once again to each other. I described the beginning of my sophomore year, adding bits he wasn't aware of. We laughed as we shared our awkward hopes and hidden longings for each other.

"You know, I hated Middlebury my freshman year," I began. "But everything changed when I met you.

"It was my black Chevy."

"You keep saying that. I was going to take the train home for Christmas break. Next thing I knew I had canceled. It was that call from Bill Joyce mentioning 'Pete Parker's car.'"

"Yeah, Bill. He knew I wanted more passengers to help pay for gas. And he knew you lived in Detroit. He liked you. I had heard your name vaguely."

"I remember you were busy arranging the suitcases in the trunk while Bill didn't budge behind the steering wheel, just like my brother George, who never would put himself out for anyone. Bill said he knew the way home to Aurora and was dying to drive. You let him. Somehow, I ended up in the back seat in the middle between you and Mary.

"You remember that?"

"We were pleasantly squeezed and jiggled against each other on those cheap seat springs. Bill was a typical alpha male, palming the steering wheel next to Peggy. All I remember is us laughing as we left the campus behind."

Peter gave Bill credit for cracking jokes. I told him my eyes were glued to the male next to me . . . him.

"I first fell in love with your blue eyes. Not even them so much as your crows' feet. They crinkled every time you laughed."

We were in our own little world rolling along oblivious to the blur of barns and snowy pastures whirling by outside. When we dropped Peggy off in Skaneateles, again, Peter got out and carried her suitcase up the front steps. Snow flurries thickened. Bill didn't move. All I remembered was how Pete, relaxed behind the driver, made me laugh. A terrific magnetism was pulling me toward him. Our thighs touched with prickling electricity.

"The funny thing is that I had no idea. I think I was guarded. You seemed pretty self-confident. I had been jilted at ASU by a girl I liked. That was another reason I wanted to transfer to Middlebury." Peter began to recall his own situation.

"Good thing. ASU was beneath you."

"Aw, sweetheart." Peter gave me a squeeze and we dropped off to sleep tangled together.

Thinking back today about that magical journey across New York state through a blizzard turning into a white-out, I knew I was in love by the time we reached Buffalo in the dark. In that car, in less than thirteen hours, I had been struck like Saul, but on the road to Detroit rather than Damascus. Pete Parker was not only physically appealing, angular, sinewy and tall, but fun, helpful, confident enough in his skin to be a passenger in his own car. After winter break, however, trying to find this man once we were back on campus was not easy. The attraction had been slightly one-way. There was no word from Pete. Two weeks passed. Slowly my heart began to bleed.

When a third week passed with no sight of the student who knew where my dormitory was, I sank into despair. My roommate Tiffany, a music major I nicknamed "Tiff" in instant affection, chose to comfort me by slipping Rachmaninoff's Second Piano Concerto out of its jacket onto her record player. It swirled our whole room into its vortex with my sobbing.

"He'll never love me. He'll never, never know I love him. Never."

Everything promising and beautiful in life was being torn at that moment from my heart and nerve center as the Concerto's famous theme, *Full Moon and Empty Arms*, mirrored my desolation. Hollywood couldn't have scripted it better.

Tiff in her quiet way soothed me, nodding thoughtfully.

"Maybe he will respond. You can't be sure."

Hearing her voice from outside my emotional gale was comforting. Her suggestion of possibility kept my small skiff from capsizing.

When a new semester started in January, I enrolled in an oil painting class. The girl sitting next to me leaned over and whispered,

"Everyone in this class is way beyond me. I feel like a klutz!"

Jo, with her owlish glasses, and I bonded over our amateur canvases. At break time she and I walked over to the student union for a cup of tea.

To my surprise, Pete Parker was sitting at a table all alone having a chocolate frappe. My heart raced. With Jo as my foil, I suggested we go over and sit with Pete. The three of us joked and laughed, and an echo of the wonderful ride to Detroit drifted back. Jo teased Pete about his sweet tooth and black Chevy. He was known to stop now and then to pick up students walking up the hill from town.

"Oh, I know all about my four-wheeled personality."

"Where are those wheels when I'm dragging back uphill to class with a load of books!"

Jo chattered, I smiled, tongue-tied. She was chummy rather than flirtatious.

Two days later we returned to the "Stu U" and to my delight there sat Pete Parker again, alone, savoring another tall chocolate milkshake. This time we went right up to his table and sat down like old friends. While Jo laughed, I was scrutinizing his behavior. Was he here for the ice cream, or possibly, just possibly, in hopes of seeing Jo and I appear this second time?

By our third or fourth trip to the café, finding Pete again at his usual table, I mustered new optimism. His glances were making longer eye contact at each visit. The next week at break time Jo waved to me to go ahead as the professor inspected her canvas. The man I was in love with was at his predictable post.

"Could we see each other this weekend?" Pete asked.

"I would really love that!" Sounding a little too eager, I added, "I mean, I think so."

My world exploded. I was blinded by euphoria. Unaware, I was stepping toward the door that swings firmly into adulthood. I rushed forward into partnering, challenge, and the security that loving and being loved offers. Not a cautionary thought spoiled my elation.

"*I love it when protagonists fall in love.*" *The Cerulean Fairy radiates.*

"*You always do.*" *The Daemon does not flinch.* "*You set yourself up for disappointment.*"

"*You prefer focusing upon the long, hard Way, Daemon. I enjoy lighter moments.*"

"*As you please. Just prepare for reversals.*"

When Peter and I finally faced each other at Lockwood's, alias *Lockjaw's* to students, we were like two torrents overflowing their banks at snowmelt. We sat at a small aisle table across from each other as waitresses brushed past us, balancing burgers on skillful arms. Classmates in booths created a background din.

"So, tell me. Why hadn't I known about you last year?" I tried to avoid blurting out anything with too much ardor.

We leaned excitedly forward over our shiny square of metal-rimmed Formica. In that cube of planetary space, cigarette smoke swirled with jukebox tunes from other tables. We didn't hear or see or smell any of it. With our torsos caught in a feedback loop, we began sharing our lives as if we were catching up after an eon of absence.

"I'm a transfer student. I never liked that community college, but that's where Vermont Academy sent me. They didn't think I was Middlebury material."

I could feel a slight hurt, a willing self-revealing in this statement.

"Your school actually told you where to apply and where you'd fit academically? That's outrageous."

I found my heart drawn to this student at a deeper level. He was trusting me with his shortcomings.

"No, they were right. I was hopeless in English and languages. I could hardly read or write. No one could figure out what was wrong with me. My dad had gone to Dartmouth and knew the headmaster of the Academy earlier as his classmate. The school took a chance on me."

At each revelation I felt increasing safety, a reassurance I'd never felt with any male my age.

"So what was it like for you at that school?"

"Well, everyone had to play football. I didn't like it. And there was always tutoring. Most of the time I felt discouraged in my classes, but I was a member of the Mountain Club. I loved being outdoors. I was a pretty good skier, but not good enough for the team.

"Oh, a skier!" I began to enhance the image of the student across from me.

"No. If you're looking for an athlete, you've got the wrong man," Pete stated matter-of-factly, to my embarrassment.

"A lot of the time I was homesick. But I knew Dad had sent me to the school to help me."

This being emerging across the table from me had the strength to state truths for better or worse. My awe intensified.

"My dad was stern but fair. We did most of the outside work around the house, keeping the big lawn mown, digging a cistern, re-roofing the garage. I was right beside him helping. He paid me. He figured I could earn a living physically if I failed at school."

Pete Parker seemed eager to share his flaws. He wanted me to know his history. Family played a strong role for him.

"And how about your mom?"

This question made my new love's eyes soften. He talked of his mother with an air of devotion, explaining her severe heart trouble. Doctors said she wouldn't live beyond twenty.

"She is the greatest person I've ever met. She may be frail, but she makes up for it in character. It's my mother that has taught me about what really matters in life."

As Pete described his parents, I sensed unusual self-assurance. He had no hidden agenda. The more he said the more my attraction grew. I tingled with the pleasing thought, "He needs my skills." Then he began to comment about human nature and life purpose and Kant's morality principle that he was learning about in a class.

"You're a philosophy major?" My heart leapt a beat. Now my new love passed into areas way beyond my reach. I suddenly looked up to this individual, feeling superficial.

"Pete, I am daunted by you."

"Don't be. I've struggled all my life in school."

"Are you kidding? You are solid and thoughtful."

The man across from me was golden-skinned, with straight hair flipping in a cowlick despite a perfectly shaped head and profile with a strong nose and angular chin. His soulful eyes searched mine for acceptance, for a spirit he could trust. His broad shoulders and muscular arms and hands looked used to hard work, his torso so long his Oxford blue shirt came untucked at the waist. I was facing an individual who had no use for embellishment or image. In contrast, my own tendency was to polish my attributes a little. Suddenly I felt shallow. My skills were mainly memorizing. I could parrot back conjugations and learn idioms.

As we gazed into each other's eyes over our empty soda glasses, *Blue Moon* was blaring above all the restaurant chatter. We didn't want the night to end. But Middlebury had a 10 p.m. curfew for women. When it came time to pay the bill, Pete gallantly pulled out his wallet, paid with a generous tip and spent no time counting change or scrutinizing for waitress errors. I mounted the steps to my dormitory in an altered state, feeling a safety with a depth I had never known. Here was a man with the grounding I lacked: calm, confident in his being if not in his verbal skills. We needed each other.

The Fairy smiles. "Take a rest, Daemon, my friend. Leave our protagonist to me for a while. You know I love lovers."

The Daemon is silent, then speaks. "Don't spoil things, Cerulea."

"You only value the tough times. She deserves this happiness."

The Daemon composes on the spot. "Recite for her this poem."

"Oh, a poem again?" Cerulea frowns but knows the

Daemon rules.
The Fairy begins half-heartedly:

Embrace your world, protagonist
Clasp shield and coat of mail
The Age of Adolescence, soon,
Brings warfare some minds fail.

Hold all that makes life worth the fight
Adulthood's risk is deep
Across a chasm there it waits
Demanding cosmic leap.

From that night on we spent every possible moment after classes together. Peter and I were in love, wildly, unreservedly. But our passion affected us each differently. A look into his smiling blue eyes drew me to a special attraction for his strong-shaven jaw. I wanted to be close to him, feel our arms touch, hold hands. One night, as he was saying goodbye on the dormitory porch on our third date, he took me by the hand and led me to the far corner out of the porch light. He pronounced jauntily, "I think we know each other well enough now," and kissed me. It was a heavenly moment. It was the first inkling I had of what was going on in his twenty-year-old body. Mine was fixed in euphoria not unlike my early enchantment with Santa Claus.

The kiss immediately promoted our intimacy to a new level. We would now discover that Peter was earthbound, and I was dreamy. The girl who lived in her imagination, poorly grounded, ever on the lookout for lofty ideals, had attracted a man whose hormones raced. It wasn't long before his hands couldn't help themselves from slipping to my breasts. This new experience, his touching the part of which I was most ashamed, attached to old guilt about being skinny, refusing to eat, made me cringe. A second later he uttered in surprise, "Why, you're almost as flat as a boy!"

I was mortified. But his surprise carried nothing more than passing curiosity. To him it was a fact, perhaps an interesting one. His response helped me take a step forward in casting off my crippling shame. What he loved in me may have been my buoyancy, a quality ingrained in his mother. He had an affection approaching reverence for this thin-framed parent. His father, on the other hand, had been an unrelenting task-master through boyhood, teaching his son to shovel coal, pile firewood. My new love had grown up with his own shame over the struggle to decipher words. Dyslexia had not yet been recognized publicly. This affliction gave him a frustration that surfaced in endearing ways.

"God damn it, how do you pronounce 'insca-, in-esca-, in-esca-pa-bly'!?" His eyes jumbled letters. "How can you love anyone who stumbles like I do. I'm stupid!"

"You're fine, you just need a secretary." I loved rescuing him with my verbal skills.

13

Destiny

The possibility of a humiliating out-of-wedlock pregnancy haunted most every college female in the 1950s, and to a lesser degree most males. Despite this taboo, a few couples found the magnetism of forbidden sex impossible to overcome, marrying, sometimes pregnant, before graduating. With strict curfews for women, colleges did their best to control the student population's sexuality, acting "in loco parentis" with house rules and parietal hours. Cars were not allowed among freshmen; most males did not have one.

I loved being close to Peter, and loved knowing I affected him potently. But his sexuality was pushing him far beyond my emotional responses. I recognized a surprising tightening up within me, an almost prudish fear. This puzzled me because everything about this wonderful partner was so genuine, spontaneous. I was in love with my man ethereally; Peter was in love with his entire self and body.

In addition, revealing something atypical if not anomalous, my psyche seemed to have cut this beautiful man in half. I loved all his maleness above the waist, his beard, deep voice, large eager hands, electrifying kisses. He possessed a lower half too, however, that he was eager to have me appreciate. I had a reaction of aversion to the genitals of the man I loved.

Dealing with so many mixed emotions, I began to draw back. This sudden cooling off, tamping down our joint eagerness, worried Peter. His intensity was stifling my playfulness. For a period, I purposely avoided his company, not ready for his seriousness. Besides, Peter was a little too predictable. Something in me wanted a little more game, a little playing at "hard to get."

Peter was not impressed with this behavior. The next time we were together he gave me a lecture.

"Love is not a power of politics, you know!" He looked at me like a parent, searching my face for the "chase" instinct he felt needed nipping.

"Let's go for a ride," I responded, feeling sheepish. I looked up to this unusual student anew; he had seen right through me. He had the maturity I longed for.

Peter, in turn, cooled to my shallow behavior. In a panic, I sensed his disenchantment. It wasn't a lover's quarrel so much as a downward adjustment of initial infatuation. There was a Steinway grand piano in our dormitory lounge. One day I had even sat down and played a short piece without anyone objecting or listening.

"Would you like me to play the *Moonlight Sonata* for you?"

I had packed my sheet music at my mom's suggestion, despite insisting it would be a nuisance with no time to pursue music classes.

"You play the piano? Fantastic!"

I gave a rusty but creditable rendition of Beethoven's pensive first movement.

"Julie, can you play it again? I can't believe you did that so beautifully."

Peter was smitten anew. He loved my creativity. I loved his grounding. We grew more inseparable than ever.

We were waltzing, however, on the edge of a turn of events neither of us foresaw.

A classmate next door, Janie, was instrumental in the throw of the fateful dice. A French major like me, she came back to her room excited one evening.

"Julie, I have just met a senior who told me about her student year in Europe last year. She said she had enrolled in the Sweet Briar College *Junior Year in France* program. It sounds out of this world!"

"What do you mean? There is a college program that exists in France?"

"There is! I met this senior in the career office yesterday. I overheard her raving about what a fabulous education the year abroad had given her. So we talked. She said it changed her life."

"Then why don't we know anything about such a year?"

"She told me outside the office that Middlebury doesn't like students to leave campus . . . they lose tuition. But she went on about how it's the only way to really become fluent in French and know the culture—actually living there."

Something like a warning shiver passed between Peter and me when I mentioned Janie's discovery. She sent off a letter to Sweet Briar College for information. Soon we were poring over the materials and application blank. Sweet Briar had initiated its year abroad in 1948, after a few other international study programs were interrupted by the Second World War. The program had established host families for all of its students, and a classroom building in Paris where it offered courses suitable to Americans developing their language skills. Credits gained during the year abroad were guaranteed transferrable.

"I'm going to do this, Julie. I'm just not inspired by our French major here at Midd."

As I imagined Janie gaining an immersion experience in the Old World, the idea grew more appealing. She would be enriching her command of the French culture beyond anything Middlebury could offer. Suddenly my French major took on a dimension of international significance. Deep in my heart I began to know I would spend that year abroad with Janie. Peter knew it too.

In his car with me, driving to Tops south of town for a hamburger, Peter tried to be generous.

"I know a year in France makes sense for your major. And yet I fear everything we have built together is going to fall apart."

I was sitting next to him with my hand on his knee, my eyes having their own love affair with his profile outlined against the front window, his angular jaw twitching nervously.

"Peter, how could our love ever change . . . you are ideal for me. There is not another man in the world that could take your place. I might have settled for lesser matches if I hadn't met you."

"That's easy to say. But think of the world you are heading into. We'll be so far apart. You'll be having all kinds of experiences that I can't share. Not only distance, but time. An awful lot can happen in a year."

"I'll be writing to you every day! That will be half the fun!"

He turned to me briefly, fixing me with a look of pain that saw tragedy ahead, squeezing all the joy out of the fragile tenderness he felt growing between us, like a seed's first tiny pair of leaves withering. "Julie, I can't bear the thought of losing you."

His clear blue eyes were pleading, making me reach over and kiss his wonderful large hand I lifted off the steering wheel.

"I feel the story of my life has been disappointment, over and over, until I met you. You accept me the way I am, unable to spell, unable to read easily."

"Peter, you're a thinker. Spelling is a skill way below the way you reflect about life and its great questions. I feel callow. I want to learn to think in France. To have a mind more like yours."

Our playfulness had turned sober. Commitment was an aspect of maturity I hadn't given any thought. Our conversations took on a weightiness that made me feel grown up. Night after night we were binding each other with unseen strings like Gulliver.

Peter began to talk about coming to see me over Christmas vacation. It soothed us but I was already under the spell of the unknown adventure to another world. My spirits rose higher and higher. I swung wildly from concern about our relationship to excitement over the coming year. The tension added high-stakes drama in the same way lovers report how war affects them when bombs are dropping all around spraying shrapnel. We headed into the hills around campus a few times, finding empty barns where we worked out the passion of the test facing us on a pile of last fall's hay, ending in tears and a wild embrace that almost broke the sex taboo. Something in me held us back, but both our natures bowed to "thou shalt not's." Peter was by nature rule-abiding.

Before the summer ended, Peter invited me to visit him in Chicago for a weekend and to meet his family. Two younger sisters were at camp as counselors. In the countryside of La Grange, a suburb with farms and great swaths of undeveloped land, I fell instantly in love with the Parkers' sprawling country home secluded from neighbors. It was all wood and French doors and patterns copied from nature. Peter's mother, tall, thin from her rheumatic heart but vibrant in voice and gestures, greeted me warmly. She had slight strabismus, having lost one eye in a childhood accident. The magic I felt for Peter now mushroomed into an embrace of everything that his parents had created together. Polished wooden floors shone around the edge of lawn-like green rugs and front windows, curtained with a crewel fabric Mrs. Parker called *Tree of Life* woven in India. The step-down family room had huge windows overlooking a vast spreading lawn with old oaks stretching horizontal limbs. Copper pots and brass vases with ferns and ivy sat on floor surfaces in a dining room bay window. The outdoors, in this home, dominated furnishings without another home in sight.

Unlike the atmosphere at my own family's dinner table, there was a lofty intellectualism in the Parker nightly conversation. Peter's father, a Unitarian with no use for anything science couldn't prove, spoke in a low, grave voice that made listeners incline inward to catch his weighty commentary on human failings. He was short and balding, with intensely piercing blue eyes that gazed at me without smiling. The world of ideas reigned at the table as he stretched forth both arms and accentuated his points like a pastor. I sensed Mr. Parker's disapproval of me, his son's vivacious girlfriend, the first intruder upon this household slightly aloof from the rest of humanity.

Early in September, after both of us finished our summer jobs, Peter drove the black Chevy from Illinois to pick me up in Detroit. As we headed for New York City, my parents excitedly waved us off, promising to visit us in Paris in springtime. Mother thought Peter was wonderful. We navigated our way to Pier 90 on the Hudson River where the Cunard Line docked its famed fleet. Janie was there, waving. Peter snapped pictures of us on deck on either side of the lifesaver-lettered "S.S. Mauretania."

As the ship chugged slowly out of New York Harbor, one heavy heart, Peter's from the quay below, and another bubbling with excitement on the high deck of a massive liner, waved goodbye to each other. We watched as our silhouettes grew smaller and smaller, becoming specks among the crowds that finally turned into a blur and vanished.

Right away Janie and I squeezed gaily into our tiny two-bunk stateroom below deck for the weeklong crossing. There were dances. A student from Yale invited me shyly when the band played a fox trot. My spirits sailed over the vast inky expanse of ocean. Feelings for Peter soon segued into a new infatuation: an eons-old continent taking shape like a phantom out of the mist. Our liner chugged slowly, silently toward its dark shoreline of Cherbourg, emerging in the predawn five days later. Tiny lights blinked and figures on the wharf scurried back and forth in pre-dawn blackness preparing for the docking. Fog horns mourned their greeting.

Land! And one not my own! It floated, smelled of strange fuel. Charcoal-burned and incendiary bombed, it was real in its own way, representing safety and rescue from something happening too quickly between me and Peter. I counted on this year to teach me to think, to grow intellectually like the man I looked up to, and to debate politics, religion, and humanity's great questions. Saboteurs lurked in me.

14

Cornered

The magic of landing in France with eighty college juniors thrust all of us into an altered reality. My nostrils flared at the pungent smells of unfamiliar fuel exhaust and primitive public toilet plumbing the day we disembarked. Small, dented buses whisked us through Norman countryside and gray stone villages huddled around a church spire toward the Loire River town of Tours. There, host families waited to greet us for our orientation program in the heart of royal chateau country dating back 700 years.

Males made up about 25 percent of our group. One was the tall, ill-at-ease student from Yale who had asked me to dance at the nightly mixers on the Mauretania. He was housed in a pension down the street from our Delestang host family on the rue Traversière. His name was Walt. I wrote Peter long detailed letters every night.

In our two-story stucco and stone-trimmed residence fronted by a high wall, we adapted to the worries of post-war France through Madame Delestang. The plump, nervous widow struggled to make ends meet as anxiety engulfed her constantly fidgeting hands. Her older son was serving in the war with Algeria; former allies Russia and the United States had begun ruffling the short stretch of peace. Her delicate younger son Michel attended classes at a local institute. We lodgers augmented her meager income but our glee, especially that of Janie's hearty laughter, lightened her gloom. She overlooked our rude, thoughtless delight in European shortages.

"Janie, have you noticed the water-repellant toilet paper?"

"Are you getting bitten in bed, like me?"

There were fleas in our mattresses and no heat. The embarrassed family fell back upon apologies instead of giving us a lecture on manners. Many parts of Tours had not been restored yet. *Quartiers sinistrés* were bombed-out sections where walls were still jagged with ceilings missing. Piles of rubble and twisted metal rested on floors sprouting weeds. It was a dark time for all of Europe.

On our way to orientation classes in French culture, Janie and I picked up Walt. He was standing on the corner in front of his pension waiting for us. He liked me. Silently falling into step, he seemed safe, an unattractive male who wouldn't challenge my sworn commitment to Peter. Overly bony and slightly hunched in his jacket, Walt had prominent teeth, blotched skin, and glasses. He chuckled to himself nervously as Janie joked about French shortages. The only thing we knew about him was his clockwork determination to meet us en route to class. One morning we spotted him hurrying, even running, on a side street toward his usual corner, apparently in order to appear casually waiting for us. We found him risible, a little pathetic.

As Halloween approached, Janie and I cooked up a plan to give a party. Madame Delestang jumped into the project promising to supply cheese and crackers if we would buy Vouvray, the renowned local wine. I borrowed a family bike and rode out into a field where on a group excursion to several chateaux we had noticed a field of giant pumpkins. The farmer was raking around this food for his livestock when I announced, "*Monsieur, je voudrais acheter une de vos citrouilles.*" He looked at me quizzically, misunderstanding at first my request to buy a pumpkin. Quickly realizing I was a foreign student in one of Tours' international programs, he began to bargain. We settled on a hefty price, "500 francs" for the most perfectly shaped of the crop, eighteen inches in diameter. In 1952, 500 francs equaled roughly a dollar, an unwieldy number later divided by 100 by government decree. The ruddy man in overalls cut it from the vine, rolled it to the side of the field and I returned later to pick it up. The Delestang family fetched it in a friend's Renault.

Walt brightened as we planned the party on our way to class. He loosened up and offered to help Janie and me carve the jack-o-lantern's three-inch-thick rind. He wanted to contribute four bottles of sparkling Vouvray and come in a cowboy costume.

On the night of the party, Janie, Walt and I welcomed a mixed group of about twenty of Michel's friends and Sweet Briar students. Madame Delestang enjoyed the festivity most of all, passing around generous plates of hors-d'oeuvre. The French were particularly impressed with the face Walt had carved into the pumpkin with its formidable rind. He, without my giving it attention, had managed to co-host our party. I described the event in detail to Peter on airmail stationery with no mention of Walt.

In less than two weeks our entire junior-year group would be transferred to Paris to be assigned new lodgings for the two-semester university year. We would be scattered all over a city with twisting, narrow streets and cul-de-sacs on both banks of the Seine. This move concerned Walt while Janie and I couldn't wait to get started on the real substance of our year abroad. One late afternoon, as the orientation classroom emptied out, Walt asked me if I'd stay for a while. He wanted to share something he loved with me. I rather liked Walt by now. His quiet way wore well. He was easy on the nerves, talking very little about himself, but appearing serious, as though needing the light-heartedness of Janie and me to relax whatever was weighing on him. The classroom had a piano in it. One professor had used it to teach us songs of the chansonniers, *Barbara* and *Il y a longtemps que je t'aime* ... ("I have loved you for so long...") These melodies aroused my emotions with their melancholia.

Walt sat down at the piano and began to play. He focused intensely, leaning over the keys as if the instrument was an extension of his life force. The classroom was deserted except for the two of us. Walt was in his element. To my surprise he was a master of the very difficult rhythms of jazz. His long fingers and prominent knuckles slid over the piano keys with a confidence I hadn't seen in him before. He became totally absorbed in playing one romantic song after another. Here was a true lover of the keyboard, freely interpreting his favorite jazz artists. As he played, sounds struck at the core of my susceptibility and something happened. A rush of magnetism, innocent but overpowering, spread from cell to cell inside me, in response to the moody melodies rising from the piano. Walt's fingers cast a spell. At the keyboard he was no longer a gangly bunch of nerves. He was suddenly an artist, thoughtful, talented, appealing.

I didn't pay much attention to my surprising response at first. We walked home together afterward, he standing outside my locked gate at dusk while I pressed the buzzer repeatedly. No one seemed in a hurry to let me in.

"I do not like this." Cerulea shivers, sensing the unforeseen.

"Easy on your wings, my friend. This is where the testing begins. No sense putting it off. Our protagonist's fate is in her hands."

The Daemon points out something the Cerulean Fairy has not observed.

"Notice this key moment and place. Our protagonist and the newcomer are Standing Before the Portal. When this

gate opens, a walk through it will launch Confrontation."
The Fairy twitches, pained.

In the next ten days, the sensation I experienced in Walt's presence increased rather than subsided. He wanted to play more for me. Where was this magnetism coming from? Walt was indeed a classmate with hidden depths, but awkward, almost an embarrassment determined to walk to class with us. Had he felt something upon first dancing with me on the Mauretania? Suddenly I saw Walt as a sensitive individual with deep reserves of talent. His blues rhythms in minor keys spread through me with a pull toward them or him that I had no control over. What was this force, where was it coming from? It was not sexual so much as synchronous, an overpowering vibration in tune with Walt, sound, instrument. Alarm set in. How could I feel this only two months after being so deeply in love with Peter? I confided to Janie this new feeling. It scared me. If it could overpower me so suddenly, quickly and unpredictably, then my safety in Peter's and my sworn commitment to each other was in danger. *I* was in danger. I could not trust myself.

Janie pooh-poohed the whole situation. "So he can play the piano. So what."

Walt, recognizing my sudden awakening to his hands on the keyboard, began to relax and share ideas. He was esthetic, reflective. The more we talked, the more he trusted me. I panicked. My receptivity intensified. The allure of a fellow junior year student was mocking the depth of Peter's and my bond with each other. My inconstancy shocked me.

Feelings for Walt, far from superficial, burrowed into my being to a soul level. This made the consequences more potentially perilous. Infidelity. Betrayal. Hurt. Loss of a love. Eventual aloneness. Yet, paradoxically, my nature was simply responding to a human being with deep rivers of talent and creativity. Walt genuinely longed to share what he loved with me. Apparently wholesome and innocent, this magnetism could not be indulged. If it was an angel, I must wrestle with it. Walt's decency became the enemy. I decided to act, to stem these feelings.

It was in this state of turmoil that I, along with our entire class of Sweet Briar students, transferred our lodgings and student lives to Paris.

Janie and I were assigned to a highly intellectual family involved in the Paris art world. The Pierre Girard family lived in a spacious left-bank apartment of the nineteenth-century Haussmann style. It was a stone's throw from both Place de Breteuil with its statue of Louis Pasteur and the metro station Duroc on the rue de Sèvres. Temporarily distracted by the enrollment process of choosing classes and figuring out the bus and subway system, Janie and I embraced the ambiance of one of the world's legendary cities.

A century of grime coated Paris apartment exteriors, railroad stations, museums, shops, churches, and the national assembly headquarters. The city spread a brooding pall over its citizens. There were still many *estropiés* who had lost limbs during World War I for whom signs on buses told us to relinquish our seats. Residents passing us on the streets looked grim; acrid smoke at sidewalk cafés curled up from everyone smoking Gaulois staining their fingers. Men coughed up phlegm, dogs defecated on sidewalks. Subway trains had the ever-present No Spitting warning, *Défense de Cracher.*

This was the adult world, I suddenly convinced myself, in contrast to America scrubbed like a rosy child. I swelled, in denial that I was that recently coddled American. Europe was soaking into me, making me feel grown-up. I came to France to learn how to think. Existentialism, even nihilism, was the topic flying from student to student as intense and bearded collegians shot arguments at each other, talked over each other, poked fingers to push their points. I embraced every concept clashing around me.

Madame Girard, Communist in theory, introduced heavy world topics at lunchtime. It reminded me of Peter's family around the table. She was an art critic writing for several newspapers. She challenged us, exposing our ignorance.

"*Vous, les Américaines, vous ne savez rien,*" she announced dismissively. "*Vous n'avez aucunes idées. Vous êtes des bébés dans la vie, ignorant votre propre politique, votre rôle nuisible mondial. Vous êtes protégées, naïves.*" I had to agree with her. We had no ideas, we were ignorant of politics, and of our negative role in the world, protected, naïve. I absorbed her Communist views like blotter paper, blaming America along with her for the Korean War.

Just as Paris was scrubbing him out of my thoughts, Walt managed to find me in our new city. Most of us were taking a class or two at Sweet Briar's headquarters on the Boulevard St. Germain. He spotted me enrolling in an immersion class there to increase my French fluency. I froze.

"Julie! Where are you living now? I have been hoping to see you for three weeks."

"Oh, Walt. I'm in a hurry right now, I can't talk."

Walt fell into step beside me as I rushed toward the metro.

The power that his presence still roused in me, now mid-November, frightened me.

"Walt, you may want to be with me. I don't want to be with you. I've promised my future to a student back home."

"That's fine, Julie. I understand. Let's just be friends."

"Friendship is impossible," I shot back. "I no longer want to see you."

Walt sensed my ambivalence.

"How about a cup of coffee near St. Germain des Prés?" He hurried along beside me as I tried to outdistance him.

"Just a quick cup at that little café up there."

"No, Walt. Leave me alone!"

Peter was excitedly planning to visit Paris over his Christmas vacation. Each letter of his, loving, eager, full of anticipation, shot a pang of guilt through me. With a stiff, unnatural resolve, I now turned upon my susceptibility for Walt, determined to excise it. The attraction was sneaking its tendrils into my promise to Peter. I must cut it.

Dark skies and chilling winds surrounded the two of us as I pushed against my feelings walking at dusk down the Boulevard. A frowning vendor roasting chestnuts watched us through squinting eyes. No, I couldn't stop for coffee, no, I didn't want to go to a Marcel Pagnol play ... stop suggesting! Walt followed me toward my *trente-neuf* (the "39") bus stop, pressing conversation. I became frantic, feeling my vacillation. Any bodily closeness to him was now terrifying me. Knowing him to be gentle and highly considerate, I felt hateful. Like a cornered feline, I turned savage. I would need to carve this insidious attraction out of me, self-mutilating. The enemy was in me, but Walt's insistence forced a turning of the scalpel on him as well.

"*Daemon my partner, I can hardly bear to see our protagonist slash away at herself so ruthlessly.*"

"*Admittedly. But remember, our protagonist longs to grow up. Notice she is choosing commitment, the basis of maturity.*"

"*But, see how she is injuring another, not only herself.*"

"*Human journeys intercept each other in endless webs of consequences. Our role is to be eternally vigilant. And detached, my friend.*"

The Cerulean Fairy wipes a tear. "*Detachment fits you better than me.*"

The next day Walt pursued me, descending a flight of stairs at Sèvres-Babylone subway, pushing through the ticket control after me, climbing on to the metro train I had decided to take home to Duroc station. He squeezed in next to me among the crush of evening Parisians heading home. Our conversation in English drew ears of a circle of eaves-droppers pretending no interest, catching a word here and there. Walt again insisted he didn't need love.

"I just enjoy your companionship. Speaking French with you. Can't we simply talk a little after class?"

"I can't. It doesn't work," I snapped, increasing the drama.

Walt was determined not to let me go; I was trying to harden. We passed my Duroc stop without moving, subway doors opening and closing, talking furiously. We came to the end of the line. Still in strong dispute, we transferred to another line. Passengers got on and off, crowding us, pressing us tightly together, pretending not to hear our heated foreign-tongue dispute. As a monotonous loudspeaker announced station after station, the train roared through dark tunnels carved into the rough bedrock under Paris. We came to the end of the second line. We transferred onto a third line. I wanted resolution. It was now pitch dark outside. We were zigzagging all over Paris from Auteuil to Nation to Porte Maillot on the subway. The more he insisted, the more I resisted. It was now approaching 8 p.m., the hour the Girard family would be sitting down for dinner. Transferring our way back to Duroc, Walt looked crestfallen. We stepped out of the train door, exited the dirty white-tiled underground passageways and mounted the stairs leading to the rue de Sèvres. The two of us walked slowly to the front door of the Girard apartment building. There in front of the double glass door he took hold of my right hand.

"Well," he said, "if this is to be goodbye, I want to do one last thing."

He pressed my right hand firmly against his genitals, bent his tall frame down to my face level and gave me a long kiss of farewell.

I said only, "Why did you hold my hand like that?"

His response was simple. "Because I didn't want you to slap me in the face."

I felt his definite erection. Confused, I bade him farewell, turned my back and pressed the bell for the concierge to unlock the door.

Crumpled from the hack job I had just perpetrated, I sat down at the Girard's table and stared silently at a lovely dinner of beef cutlets in wine gravy. A lump in my throat made it hard to swallow the creamed leeks. Another letter from Peter had been waiting on the Girard's hallway table, easy to identify with its light borders of diagonal *par avion* slashes. It was full of excited questions about our upcoming plans for our two holiday weeks together and the thrilling details of his plane flight from Montreal to Paris. There would be refueling stops in Gander and Shannon, Ireland. How many days would we stay in Paris? Would we go to Austria to ski as well? What town should we spend Christmas Eve in . . . how about Innsbruck? Janie would come with us, of course. Peter was studying the map of Europe, investigating the train system. Life took a dark turn that night for me. I was frozen with fear.

15

Self-Damning

At the appointed morning hour, in dread, I closed the heavy front portal of the Girard's apartment behind me and walked to the Duroc metro station to board the subway train. Peter would by now have landed at Orly Airport and had been instructed to take the metro subway to the station most convenient to our 7th arrondissement, the Gare des Invalides. There was no easy communication in those days to assure waiting greeters that a plane had touched down.

As I walked toward the wide stairs that led down to the trains, I spotted Peter, almost alone at that moment, rushing up the stairs upon spotting me, arms outstretched, his face overjoyed. Something inside me shrank. I put on my best smile, masking betrayal. He swept me into his arms with a long embrace, soon talking excitedly about his flight from Montreal.

"I drove the black Chevy from Middlebury north across the border and parked in the outside lot. Then I boarded Canada Airlines in the evening." His eyes sparkled with excitement as he recounted a bit of history.

"We stopped at Gander in Newfoundland. What an arctic land-scape. You know that's the same runway used by 20,000 Canadian and

American fighter-bombers who landed to refuel during World War II. And here I am a few years later coming to visit my girlfriend!" He threw his arm around my shoulder and bent down to peck my cheek.

We climbed onto the metro toward *Duroc*, Peter maneuvering a suitcase among the crowds of rush-hour morning commuters jostling us. It was magical for him. Soon we were at *Duroc*, me stepping off the train with him following, and mounting the subway stairs to the walk toward our apartment building. Everything for him was strange, worthy of commentary. As Monsieur Girard opened the door for us, Madame Girard was there to greet us. Janie gave him a boisterous welcome. Peter made an instant hit with the Girards. They had prepared a cot for him in a small library room off the dining room. As we sat down for a noon dinner, Peter hurried around the table to pull out the dining room chair to seat Madame Girard.

"Peter, that's not the custom here," I said a little too quickly. Madame Girard reprimanded me.

"*Laissez-le, c'est charmant. Je l'aime bien, cette coutume.*" Peter became persona grata right away. Madame Girard found the gesture charming.

After the first morning waking up in our hosts' apartment, Peter was naturally eager to find a corner where the two of us could be alone. This was the moment I most feared, stealing glances at his eyes shining with anticipation. After breakfast of toast and apricot marmalade, we headed over toward St. Germain des Prés Cathedral on the metro to find a simple table in a café where we could share "state-of-the-heart" feelings.

My Paris world clustered around the historic quartier where the rue de Sèvres meets the Boulevard St. Germain. Parisians poured in and out of the Café de Flore glaring and arguing or at the equally famous Deux Magots at classy little tables in a haze of smoke. We couldn't afford those holy abodes of Sartre and Simone de Beauvoir. We were the students reading their celebrated works in class, even seeing Sartre's latest play, *Huis Clos,* on cheap tickets in my French Drama seminar.

Peter and I looked for a homey brasserie, passing a patisserie en route. He lingered over the endless rows of berry tarts, *babas au rhum* (rum-soaked yeast cakes) and chocolate éclairs, so we went in for a closer look. He bought us each a confection with my dollar-to-franc conversion help. Walking along, sampling bites of each other's buttery shells, we found a corner bistro and took refuge from the noise and gloomy winter day. The cafe door closed out the distraction of street fumes and Renaults honking in a traffic snarl. No buffer now separated us. Peter sat down across from me at a small round table as hot chocolate arrived. He reached for my hands and looked at me, eyes alight.

"How are you, my dearest?" The moment of truth had arrived. I looked down, then sideways, feeling my forehead tighten, my brow wrinkle. I could not lie to this authentic man.

"Well, I have something to share with you." I glanced at him quickly, then looked away.

His face fell. "What?" he asked, alarmed. He pulled his hand back.

"Well," I continued, searching for how to express something in the least hurtful way to him, least damaging to me.

"I sort of fell for a student here with us in our Sweet Briar group. But it's over now," I added a little too hastily. "I mean I am getting him out of my system. I never want to see him again."

Thunderstruck, Peter stared at me. He didn't understand what I had just said. His eyes searched mine, squinting.

"You mean you've fallen in love with someone else?"

I lamely corrected him. "It wasn't falling in love. It was a crush. It was just, well, I don't know what it was. It's you that I love. I never want to see him again."

The misery intensified. Peter continued to look at me. He might have been thinking, "No. This has happened to me too many times before." Whatever his sense of shock was, it turned him immediately to steel.

I had hurt him, and his instinct was to armor himself in return. We became, at that table, sudden strangers to one another, pretending to onlookers that all was well. When we got up, paid the bill and walked out onto the boulevard, our love had changed. All charm vanished. We were a pair of college students, miserable and disillusioned, stuck in France to make the best of the next two weeks. Outwardly in the most romantic situation imaginable, we sank into anguished silence and put on masks with painted smiles. We proceeded on our itinerary pretending nothing had changed.

The magic of Austria's sheer mountain precipices and tiny villages distracted us. On Christmas Eve, in the hush of alpine Innsbruck we walked through the village square with its giant Tannenbaum fir lit with tiny glowing candles. A light blizzard blurred the last few hurrying shoppers in the dusk, leaving their footprints on snow in a grey and white tableau of a silent village emerging from war. With Janie we had our own little holiday celebration in our *Goldener Stern* Inn, exchanging presents and pretending to be jolly in the room she and I shared. Over the next two days, Peter and I found our way to the famous *Nordkette,* Innsbruck's local "jewel of the alps," where we took the tramway up the mountain and skied. I found a beginner's slope and joined him at the end of the day. Peter was sinewy and angular, a competent skier who had strong endurance for outdoor sports, especially mountaineering requiring ropes and crampons. The Alps awed him; he resolved to enjoy his vacation rather than fixate on a disappointed heart.

By the end of our two weeks together Peter and I had settled into acceptance of our inner states like wounds we tried not to pick at. My love for Peter had developed a sore in meeting Walt. I had tried to excise the sore, and it would take time to cover over with new skin. In the healing, however, my feelings, originally so spontaneous for all that seemed wholesome and beautiful and admirable in our world, developed scar tissue. Never again would I feel that uninhibited flood of ecstasy that had made me tingle at Peter's every kiss and caress. I longed for its return for decades.

After parting with forced cheerful goodbyes, Peter flew back to Middlebury for exams before a second semester. I returned to my Paris apartment shaken. What lay ahead? I knew cognitively that I loved him but wondered if his love for me could surmount betrayal. We continued to write to each other using endearing words but mention of commitment had vanished. His letters were full of campus life news and closed routinely with how much he missed me. Mine pictured student life in Paris, small trips and interesting new acquaintances. I began to share with him the papers I was writing for classes, exploring philosophical aspects of an author's levels of meaning.

A French veterinarian student that Janie and I had befriended, Philippe Dewailly,[6] knew our student year was ending. We three became like siblings, companions free of emotional entanglements. I had performed such savagery upon my instincts of attraction that never again would I stray into dangerous or even harmless infatuations. Philippe held unorthodox views about medicine and practiced yoga, a word new to me, in great solemnity. Once in a joint horseback riding outing in the Bois de Boulogne, he had demonstrated an impressive yoga headstand on horseback, his hands braced on the saddle of his mount. I was a doubter by nature, attending Sunday school in a liberal Congregational Church, influenced by Mother who loved reciting passages from Ecclesiastes: *"Man has no advantage over the beasts, for all is vanity."*

One day Philippe and an ailing friend asked if I would like to go along to witness a session with a psychic the friend had engaged, joking that it might erase my skepticism. In the suburbs, in the back yard of

---

6 Docteur Philippe Dewailly became one of Paris's leading veterinarians, caring for the pets of movie stars and government officials, authoring seven books on dog, cat and bird care. He has been a lifelong friend, still alive at this printing. His most recent publication, not yet in English, is *Si vous saviez ce que les animaux m'ont appris (If You Knew What Animals Have Taught Me.)* Paris, Editions Glyphe, 2021 (available on Amazon.com)

a humble dwelling, a fragile young woman was led out, eyes darting about and blinking like a wild child. Reclusive and genuine, anchored weakly in this world, she did what she was told by her "protectors." She sat down at a small table, held the hand of Philippe's friend, went into a trance and proceeded to stream revelations of healing techniques that made no sense to me but made the two men nod excitedly. When she had finished, Philippe suggested that I sit down before she emerged from her altered state to see what she might say to me. Guarded, I agreed. The psychic held my hand for a long while in silence, then made one comment. It took me by surprise.

"*Elle est morte jeune.*" "She died young." The gauzy being was then guided back inside and we returned to Paris. Her remark tucked itself into my memory, four French words with puzzling significance.

Exposure to the French culture and its professors was awakening a powerful thinking process in me. These rapidly maturing analytical powers provided a new way of connecting with Peter. I felt at last that I was "growing up," freed from Mother's efforts to keep me "playing dolls and earning Scout badges." I wanted Peter to be proud of me. Studying literature, poetry and history presented a passionate new platform for ideas as did simply being in France, the home of Descartes, Montaigne, Voltaire, Camus.

In the spring semester, I registered for a class in phonetics at the Institut de Phonétique, part of the Université de Paris in its own once-private historic chateau up a high flight of stairs. In class we all held mirrors in front of our mouths and followed Madame Leon's instructions, "*allongez les lèvres*" and "*serrez la gorge.*" Project your lips forward! Tighten your throats! I knew I was making progress when Monsieur Girard lamented, "*O, vous perdez votre charmant petit accent américain!*" He did not want to see us lose our charming American accents.

My essays were earning me sixteens and seventeens out of a score of twenty, returned full of scribbled corrections. But a sixteen was considered an achievement. Like tea leaves in cups of hot water, the longer we stayed in France the more steeped we became in it. Life in the United States could only recede like the lost continent of Atlantis before such an onslaught of stimuli. It was affecting us each in different ways. Janie began to make plans to return to Paris to job seek after her Middlebury graduation. Walt continued to phone me at the Girards in unending vain hope. At each of his attempts I became crueler, insulting him sarcastically then recoiling in horror at my monstrousness. When he discovered the return date of my ship passage, he made a reservation to sail on the same ship. It would have been a final torture had not his mother died unexpectedly, obliging him to fly home early.

Mentally I was alive with intellectualism; emotionally I was numb, suspended in the present with no idea of what my future held. Peter floated about in that vagueness, connected to me by nothing more than year-old promises and letters increasingly mechanical.

Janie and I celebrated our year together with one last short train trip, passing through Belgium to the Low Countries after our exams ended. She would stay on to travel; my parents had asked me to come home to take a summer job. The Queen Mary had an affordable berth for me on its lowest deck. With the seemingly innocuous act of my buying that one-way ticket, I fell into the hands of destiny.

Four years had now elapsed since I had come home, discharged from Forest Hospital in June of 1960. My confidence soared as I returned from my parents' home in Detroit, victorious at last with one-year-old Celeste in my arms, uniting our fragmented family in time to celebrate Christmas. A beautiful stretch of contentment unfolded in our York Road home. The worst that can possibly happen had happened. Having risen out of it, I anointed myself an emerging voice with a story that might one day be worth telling. My reward for now was in celebrating the humblest acts in normal life—lacing a child's shoe, closing a window against rain, peeling an apple. That old euphoria that had whooshed me skyward upon meeting Peter returned in tempered form. I was starting over, with scars I was proud of.

Just before her death, Peter's mother, aware of my college year in France, had made a thoughtful introduction. She had asked a friend of hers who traveled abroad frequently if it might be appropriate to invite a young mother, her new daughter-in-law, to a meeting of the local French Club. A group of educated women gathered monthly, rather exclusively, to maintain their conversation skills. Approval for membership depended upon the level of one's linguistic fluency and "fit" among the genteel owners of Chicago's western suburbs' finer homes. Upon my acceptance, I not only found a warm connection between two continents whose trench I had not yet bridged, but I encountered an individual who was to influence my future in ways I could not imagine at age twenty-six.

She came up to me quietly smiling, hesitating as the other ladies bee-lined toward the dining room table, set with a shining silver tea set surrounded by plates of cupcakes and finger sandwiches. I hadn't noticed her among the well-groomed matrons rushing forth to greet me and assess my French. Where had I learned my nearly flawless accent? What was my alma mater? They were like zinnias in a garden, all branching from the same stem. She, on the other hand, approached me shyly in their shadow, a delicate fringed lily. I was captivated. What was it that I felt in her presence, maybe a hidden pool, maybe suffering in that countenance? In gentle, almost muted French, she spoke.

"*Vous avez passé une année en France? Moi, j'ai grandi à Paris.*" (You've spent a year in France? I grew up in Paris.)

As she looked at me without any nervous glancing sideward typical of first meetings, her gaze had a self-effacing gravity. Her loveliness was not so much physical as ethereal. Standing in her presence, I felt that same tenderness toward her that had drawn me to my father early in life, a vulnerability. She was about my height and stature, with waves of brunette hair circling Irish-white skin and deep blue eyes.

Her name was Louise. We shared bits about ourselves in French. Her father had been appointed minister of the American Church in Paris during her youth, so she attended primary school there until crossing the Channel to a strict girls' school in England predating World War II. At eighteen, she had arrived on U.S. soil for the first time to attend college. She was fourteen years my senior but looked youthful, almost contemporary.

As we talked and smiled at each other, I wondered if she might be willing to explore a friendship. I came home eager to share my enthusiasm.

"Peter, I met an unusual member at the French Club today. She is quite a bit older than we are, but I was drawn to her. Do you suppose we might invite Louise and her husband to dinner?"

"Why not? What is her husband's name?"

"I'm not sure, Bob, I think. Their two children are teenagers."

"Well, we have sort of mix and match furniture, but if that matters to them, we won't click anyway."

We were so much younger, and again, so much less urbane, it seemed, that I felt awkward and worried they would say no. Everything "Louise" was a new enchantment. I gathered courage to call the couple, bracing for their decline. Louise said they would love to come. She needed to check with her husband's schedule.

I was ecstatic. Louise's thoughtful poise had immense appeal, worlds apart from my own blurting spontaneity.

At that first dinner I waited anxiously to hear steps on the porch. When I welcomed them in with nervous chatter, Louise sat down gingerly on the durable sofa-bed behind the oval pine coffee table. Bob leaned back in one of the stiff curved-wood captain's chairs from Great Aunt Nellie's attic and crossed a knee in comfort. The two antiques I had repainted glossy black creaked a little, either side of our fireplace. Bob made polite conversation while Louise, in a soft blue skirt and sweater, smiled at all of us, radiating a mystique that brushed our whole living room with magic. I stole glances at her, as if she lived in a secret world I might enter if invited. Bob, relaxed and self-composed, took a pipe out of his pocket, unlit at first. When Peter brought drinks and the two men talked of military life, he waved it for emphasis, with an air of distinction. We were captivated as he talked about his war years "flying the hump" over Burma.

As I served popcorn after burning one batch and succeeding with a second when Bob suggested a spoonful of oil might help, Louise talked with a voice almost weightlessly musical about her life before they arrived in the Chicago suburbs. She recounted her life before marrying, before arriving in America. I parsed her every word for a fragment that might reveal her mysteriousness as she related tales of her English preparatory school.

"We girls were never warm enough," she stated simply. "Our uniforms were too thin. The winters in those dormitories were so dank and shivery that we all had chilblains. I got tuberculosis."

Louise talked in short phrases, describing her youth calmly, as if facts of no consequence.

"When I was sent to the sanatorium for a year my mother didn't come to visit me once." She added, "Every time a visitor was announced I was sure it would be my parents. It never was." In quiet tones she spoke as if describing a weekly trip to the library, but sought my eyes, activating my rescuer tendency.

I couldn't bear to think of this lovely new friend suffering. She shared her longing to be home in France with her family, but her mother, thanks to her husband's position, was a kind of "grande dame" that whirled about the countryside buying French antiques and art objects. Aversion rose instantly in me to this imagined maternal figure.

By the end of the evening, Peter had conversed with Louise's husband about both of their manufacturing companies in Chicago while Bob puffed on his lit pipe with little popping sounds. He was tall and gallant that evening, apparently at ease with his greenhorn hosts. Inhaling the sweet smell of pipe smoke trailing behind Bob as the door closed behind them, I sang with joy, dishwashing, over the promise of a charmed new friendship.

Louise's seniority and reserve kept me at a reverential distance. But she and Bob soon invited us to have dinner with some of their friends. I observed their sophistication watching Bob offer an array of cocktails favoring Manhattans, and Louise presenting an assortment of hors d'oeuvre. But Louise was enigmatic. As we grew closer, she revealed one afternoon that she had been very ill when she first arrived in the Chicago area. I inquired exactly what had been the cause. She stated simply,

"I had a nervous breakdown."

Stunned, and at the same time feeling a burst of pleasant surprise at the thought this special individual and I had something in common, I looked at her and shook my head slowly to honor her disclosure.

"Louise, I have had one too."

A special tie developed between us from that moment, although in my eyes Louise belonged to a world just beyond reach. I longed to know more about what gave her that mysterious quality. I might acquire a little of it.

The French Club provided the perfect bonding terrain for the two of us newcomers. As our trust in each other grew, a foundation began to solidify in my young adult life in which France was a signature ingredient. Louise and I often chose to chat in French. Conversing in those melodious syllables lifted us slightly out of the humdrum of our days, and honored the country that had played a role in both our illnesses. France held a key, even if a partial one, to how and why my mind's cohesion had failed. The idea of a return to that country in search of the cause was about to bud.

PART THREE

California
1965-1980

The faint beginnings of insight start after a gift from Louise. Escapism vies with a search for meaning through exuberant ambition: authorship. Relapse accompanies shakeup. Enter India.

16

The Unforeseen

"Peter, this could be the family trip of a lifetime! We'd revisit France with our girls for an entire summer!" My ardor was spattering about like the fat from the hamburgers I was frying.

Peter had tossed down the *Daily News* on the sofa bed, hoping for a moment to read it later as he came into the kitchen to help cut beans and slice tomatoes. Not quite five-year-old Celeste was setting the table with two forks for some and three spoons for others.

"Wait a minute. What?" He came to my side and raised his brows at me. I threw my arms around his neck and danced my eyes in a way that disarmed him.

Like spontaneous combustion, the allure of a summer return to Europe had burst into flame. I was entering a period of wild inspiration. Peter questioned, but usually went along with my brainstorms.

The idea was not outlandish. Our daughters were in a lovely period of growing self-sufficiency. Their interests had expanded, they entertained each other, and made friends in kindergarten, first and third grade. With Celeste now almost five, in school with her sisters for three hours before lunch, I had a stretch of time to myself. My imagination zoomed to France. I felt a sudden longing to return to that country while it still held remnants of Old-World magic.

"You could join us for as many weeks as you could request leave from work."

I set the scene as a mother and daughters' journey with the hope Peter would come along.

"We can visit regions I've never been to, circling from Brittany down the west coast southward to the Pyrenees, then through Provence eastward toward the Alps and north, ending in Paris. Paris, Peter! The city of my heart! What do you think?"

Peter did not share my idolization of the country I had come home from, damaged. He played the heavy, the pragmatist, more aware of my capriciousness now.

"How long do you see this trip lasting?"

"I think we'd need eight weeks at least."

"A whole summer? And how would you and the girls get there? You know I would have trouble joining you for more than a month." This comment was a sign of encouragement.

"We could book passage on a ship, maybe a Cunard line." My mind was racing.

"Then we could rent a car and drive through the countryside. Medieval towns with walls! We could tour the France I didn't really explore as a student. We'd talk with farmers and villagers, getting to know the genuine people."

"Do you really picture driving around France alone until I can join you?" My mate was on alert. "It sounds risky. And expensive. Have you thought about the cost?"

The France project swelled in my head. I burned vegetables, distracted by that question repeatedly. Where could the money come from for this fantasy? It might cost a fourth or a fifth of Peter's annual salary. The challenge inspired me. I had a degree from Middlebury with a skill that I'd never had time to practice. I would offer French classes! Yes. But, how?

One hurdle after another collapsed before my zeal. I would not teach through the community night school where my limited free time would never fit an institution's scheduling. No. I would set up my own private school. Peter watched as this fantasy wove its way around convention's normal channels. The world of historic France that I had loved was fast fading; I wanted our girls to see it, experience its crumbling charm before it succumbed to malls with their smothering sameness, Walmarts à la française.

Western society was enjoying a stretch of uneventful optimism in the early 1960s.

The word "protest" had not entered the American lexicon. We were reading in our daily paper about a new era of French productivity replacing pessimism. It would later be called *les Trente Glorieuses*, the Thirty Glorious Years that injected new faith in the French into their resurgent economy.

Peter's confidence was expanding as he rose up the ladder with bolstered engineering skills to design improvements to his company's mechanical and hydraulic lifting equipment. My hospitalization had faded to a memory almost dreamlike. Recovery had brought the return of functioning to all but my sexuality and capacity to feel deep emotion. The FDA had recently approved the contraceptive pill after fumbling a first release limited to "severe menstrual cramps." Five years later, over six million women were using it, I among them. I still wasn't much of a sex playmate, but the pills helped avoid the hated diaphragm. I delighted in life's simplest acts, reading the girls a story, singing them to sleep, weeding our tulip bed.

At French Club I met Yvette, a newcomer married to an American, who shared her struggle with the careening pace of U.S. life.

"J'ai la sensation de chasser un train qui me laisse toujours en arrière."

I felt sad for Yvette, unsmiling, feeling our U.S. culture was a train she could never quite catch. She was pale and withdrawn, her brunette hair in a typical French pageboy cut, struggling with anxiety. I invited the couple to an awkward dinner. Her husband was so stiffly silent that in my mind he was part of Yvette's problem. Shortly after that evening, she vanished, abandoning all of us at French Club.

We had joined the Hinsdale Unitarian Church, Peter's family's affiliation, which meant casting off, in exchange for science and rationalism, the tender feelings I had had as a child in the sanctuary of our Congregational Church. I suddenly scorned organized religion and any ritual requiring parroting a creed, to Peter's approval. I became a more orthodox non-believer than I had ever been a Congregationalist. It wasn't a big shift. My own family had never discussed beliefs or theories despite their regular attendance at North Congregational. For Mother, it seemed part of her routine, like trips to the beauty salon. My father, on the other hand, looked upward when singing hymns in the pew, as if joining a host of angels.

The planning stage for the trip to France began immediately. Diane and Katherine were in school from 8 a.m. to 3 p.m., but Celeste's kindergarten gave me only free morning hours Monday through Friday. Now our membership as regular Unitarians on the greeting committee paid dividends. The Hinsdale Unitarian Church Sunday School rooms sat idle most of the week. I could use the high school lounge rent-free. Church members were interested. I needed to attract a Tuesday group of intermediates with rusty grammar and a Thursday group of beginners in love with the world's most romantic language. France was becoming a popular travel destination as it cast off the shadows of war.

Diane sensed something big was afoot. I heard her whisper to Katherine.

"Mama has a new job. She is talking about a trip that we are all going on, far away."

I designed two-color posters, lettering in days, times, fees, location and my phone number. *Julie Parker, diplomée de Middlebury College,*

Université de Paris, la Sorbonne, Institut de Phonétique. The bio looked substantial. I posted one on the bulletin board of Hinsdale's main supermarket and another in the Unitarian church lobby. By dividing each of the next two years into four eight-week sessions with enrollees paying $25 a session, I calculated earnings of $1,400 to $1,600.

Peter could see the puzzle pieces of this voyage snapping together. He hugged me as he presented me his Christmas gift of the 1965 edition of the red Guide Michelin, in whole-hearted support of his partner's venture. I studied hotel prices. We could book passage out of New York harbor in a four-bunk-bed cabin on the lowest deck of the S.S. United States for $500. Then would follow seven weeks in inns as we advanced from village to village along our circular pilgrimage. *Demi-pension* in a double-bedded room in the tiniest hotel fit our budget. My energy was electric as I penciled our itinerary onto the huge map of France spread out on our living room floor. We would need to rent a car. One thousand dollars of my earnings was committed before I had the first student response.

Peter's investment in the project picked up as phone calls came in from potential students.

"You know what, Julie? Volkswagen has just come out with a new model they call a "Squareback." It's almost ready for export. I think we could have Germany deliver one to the dock in France . . . Le Havre is it . . . when your ship pulls in."

"You mean, so the car would be waiting for us when we arrive?"

"And you could drive it until I join you, then we could ship it home as a used vehicle, avoiding import duty." The idea cemented Peter's backing.

Within a month of sorting student callers into appropriate levels, I had filled two classes.

Each had fewer than the seven or eight I needed, but interest could grow by word of mouth. I planned to have fun with this group, some hesitant, some assessing me coolly over the phone. I chose books and reviewed my Language Teaching Methods course at Middlebury.

One day at French Club, Yvette reappeared after a year's absence. She looked so radiant we hardly recognized her, no longer the inhibited, spiritless French wife that had vanished.

"*J'ai découvert le yoga!*" she said, beaming. She had discovered yoga. "*Cela m'a fait énormément de bien.*" I could see she had benefited greatly from it.

We soon began to adapt to this charismatic version of the former Yvette. It was the second time I had encountered the word "yoga." My veterinarian student friend Philippe had shown me yoga postures in France, standing on his hands on horseback. He welcomed beliefs I found fringy, like the power of homeopathy and a sixth sense in animals. "Yoga" was strange-sounding, gurgling as it passed through the throat. Its power to transform Yvette puzzled me, then faded from curiosity under the avalanche of trip preparations.

Like a puzzle's empty center filling in with new pieces each day, our trip took form. I guided my women students methodically and laughed with them in the church basement over their errors or my own. The two years slipped by as I taught my subject merrily, entertaining them with tales of my student blunders learning French in Paris. These new friends fanned the flames of anticipation, traveling vicariously with me and three small children.

As my spirits soared, the original goal resurfaced. I would keep a journal and turn the adventure into a story! Not a travelog so much as an inner search for that confident vigor lost in France after I had waved goodbye to Peter from the ship deck. An idea was taking shape of my illness possessing meaning, a meaning that I could shake loose like an apple by tackling every branch of France for the one limb holding the answer. Louise and other friends in the French Club watched the intensity of my plan unfold, shaking their heads. Was I heading myself into another bout of illness?

At the end of two years, I had saved $1,500. Peter would join us in upland Auvergne after the completion of the first half of our itinerary. I hardly noticed the world was changing. President Kennedy had been assassinated. The Civil Rights Movement was awakening America. Women's Liberation was a phrase appearing in news articles. My mind was focused on socks and underwear changes in our four suitcases. They would accompany one adult and three sisters ages, ten, eight, and six, from the train to New York City, onto the ship, then into the Volkswagen Squareback waiting for us, if all went well. Then would follow seven weeks unpacking and repacking every few days, progressing to a neighboring historic province. What life would be like upon the return from this magical journey, I never gave a thought.

At this moment, through the front door one evening, into our sparse living room with its pine sofa bed, Peter entered with an out-of-the-blue announcement. Our familiar world, the one we would leave and the one we would return to at the end of the European journey, suddenly fractured into a hall of mirrors.

"Are you ready for this, Julie?" When Peter called me Julie, what followed was serious. He stood at a distance, more erect than usual, his shoulders minus their usual forward bend to meet my head, seven inches below his. "Can you picture what life would be like in California?"

I sat down and waited. "California?"

"The company has bought a small manufacturing firm in Los Angeles that makes custom-designed hydraulic equipment. The president wants me to become its manager. He asked if we would be willing to move to Southern California to see if it suits us."

Peter and I looked at each other. Our minds momentarily jammed, as if being handed meaningless wood letter squares in Scrabble. Soon word patterns appeared. The acquisition was known for its new product development projects, Peter explained. It meant a big promotion for him. In my highly-charged state, I was not able to grasp the massiveness this change suggested. France had spirited me away a second time on wings of the old student-year-abroad euphoria. I felt ready for anything, blind to consequences. Still, the land of Hollywood? We Chicagoans scorned glitzy Los Angeles "way out there," tipped westward to collect America's rolling "fruits and nuts."

I visualized a sprawling, tasteless Mecca drawing rootless hopefuls to the film world.

Peter pictured the Sierra Nevada mountain range beckoning him up 13,000-foot summits and Mt. Palomar. He had begun making a telescope at the age of twelve whose mirror he hoped to finish one day.

"Well, it sounds as if we can come home if we don't like it." With that observation, I approved the announcement jauntily and returned to the map in the living room. Peter's mind was elsewhere.

Besides plans for a European summer, I now added challenges of who might take over the French classes that were attracting next fall's students. We would need to rent out our home, again for the third time, as we tried life in Southern California. I shared the news of our move at the next French Club gathering.

"Julie, j'aimerais bien te servir comme remplaçante l'année prochaine."

With that offer, Yvette revealed her eagerness to become my substitute for the coming year. Among my last activities in Hinsdale, I met with her to transfer student information, syllabus, lesson plans, textbooks, and endless auxiliary materials I had gathered over two years. Yvette was a tie to both the French Club and the adult language students. They had become friends in the Illinois that we were about to bid farewell.

The one I would miss most, however, would be Louise. My love for her had a one-way luster to it; Louise liked me a lot, but I worshipped her. She had a mystique I longed for. I would grieve, having no idea that one day she would stun me, in California, in a particular short note that would change my life.

The summer in France was a highlight for our young family that influenced not only my future but also the trajectories of three small sisters who eventually made choices when they reached college age. I kept a daily journal. With our new super-8 camera I filmed the girls interacting with children on playgrounds or beaches, families on vacation, farmers and widows gardening in *sabots*, wooden shoes. We met Peter in the remote town of St. Flour, with me behind the wheel of our new red Volkswagen just as planned. My thrill at our reunion, along with the joy of our daughters, was reminiscent of my first encounter with their father in the black Chevy driving home from Middlebury.

In a squeaky upstairs hall drawer, undisturbed for decades, rests a tattered manila envelope. Its contents were created on my 1966 electric typewriter, a prize gift from Peter when we first moved to California. Inside the folder, in ink-ribbon letters biting into the onionskin pages, there is an unpublished manuscript that was my first attempt at a full-length memoir. I titled it *The Return of the Foreigner*.

Parkers in Paris, 1966

17

Alien World, 1966

Was it the relentless sun that made southern California so mind-numbing that fall of 1966, in our tiny, rented ranch house in Whittier? Or was it the rows of cookie-cutter structures along treeless streets with names like Portada Drive instead of York or Washington? The cloudless skies hovered over all the unattached and newly arrived on the desert below, with a mushroom-white wash that never cleared into radiant blue after a storm. That was it, at least partially. Our new world had no spirit-lifting azure dome overhead. The sky turned the Los Angeles basin paste-colored. We moved about in a semi-invisible vapor, half exhaust-pipe smoke, half fog. I longed for blue, cerulean sky blue.

The lawn of our miniature rented dwelling was of dichondra, a tiny circular leafed ground cover that sprouted slime overnight. The teachers who had rented us their snug two-bedroom, one-story house while on sabbatical had instructed us not to interfere with the Japanese gardener. The swimming pool was our responsibility. We engaged a young program director from the local YMCA to give our girls swimming lessons. The constant moisture from the chlorinated surface wafted into our family room, turning curtains into damp folds of mold. Two trees delighted us, however, with white waxy blossoms creating a spicy-sweet fragrance. They produced a marvel: oranges growing on a real stem with hearty forest-colored leaves.

Our daughters had not been consulted about a move to the West Coast. It was an uncertainty I imagined we could try for a year before returning to familiar Hinsdale. "It's only temporary," I kept telling them and myself. Diane had just turned ten; Katherine was eight and Celeste was not quite seven. With France absorbing me, I had given this trial year following the summer hardly a thought. I had no transitioning plan for our little girls. Peter brought home maps of the peaks he had climbed with his father and sisters as a teenager. He couldn't wait to schedule trips to visit Mt. Hood, climb Mt. Whitney, then explore Yosemite and local mountain ranges two hours away.

While I had no particular employment organizing my day in Whittier, our three daughters were enrolled immediately in grade school. I watched them head off together in the baking September sun to elementary school and felt their resistance to this new setting. Diane's best friend Christopher was back home; Katherine was miles from her little Hinsdale buddy Jamie, and Celeste snapped a book shut when a teacher, who called me in for a conference, tried to help her read. The sisters had returned from a far-off world to land in this strange patch of chaparral. Devil's grass punctured their bicycle tires. They whimpered over the dramatic shift in terrain.

Peter, for the first time in his married life, celebrated his new work situation. He enjoyed renting a home with no maintenance worries. He was under-studying the man in charge of the newly acquired firm to assess where he could tap its potential. This transitional role placed him among once blue-collar self-made equals, no longer under the aegis of his socialite uncle's Chicago management. He had never liked the pressure of sales calls and trade shows where drinking got out of hand.

Now, everything about the West Coast and its mountains called to him the way Europe called to me. He planned weekend trips to the ocean at Laguna Beach and to the San Jacinto mountains. It was his turn to soar, as his wife soured. He joined the local Mt. Wilson Observatory Association as an amateur astronomer. He orchestrated a family visit to Mt. Palomar and the 200-inch telescope. I could feel him falling in love with California.

With Peter heading off to work every morning and the girls in school, I picked up my notes, written daily throughout our adventures in France, in a loose-leafed binder. Frayed at two corners, that journal had traveled with us faithfully from village to village as the story grew nightly. I was sure *The Return of the Foreigner* would find a readership. The goal I had first envisioned—exploring how a year in France might have initiated mental illness—had given way to a more prosaic travel journal describing the challenges of squiring three small children, cramped in a Volkswagen, around a country on a scale half the size of America's. Villages had little fenced-in squares where a swing was a rarity.

The chapters drew me into an imaginary French womb like a fictional pregnancy, growing daily more viable. My notes electrified me, competing with greeting the girls after school or thinking about what I'd feed us for dinner. I wrote about our daughters dashing about in inn dining rooms, attracting local families whose kids came back the next day to loan them their bicycles. I remembered striding up with a friendly "Bonjour" to a shepherd in Roquefort pastures tending his sheep. He had asked why I was traveling alone with three children but no man. I responded audaciously.

"I have returned to France to discover its role in my nervous breakdown after a student year here."

Baffled, he returned to his flock in silence. While I was engaged in my own little experiment of connecting with locals to overcome the outsider I was, the villagers shuffled their feet in awkwardness. The

French are reserved around strangers. A young mother trotting about the countryside, approaching people in hamlets or fields in their own tongue, fit their familiar categorization of neither "gypsy" nor "tourist."

Recovery had led to a heady new sense of myself as vanquisher, as belonging to a select group of the tested who could adventure anywhere.

I inflated more and more with the manuscript project, sending off several chapters to a popular American literature professor at Middlebury. He wrote back with compliments, then pointed out several shortcomings. *"You referred a few times to some kind of catastrophe, but you didn't describe it in depth. We want to know more about it. Your story really is more of a "travels with Julie" than a deep exposé of mental illness."*

The academic was right. I was a novice penning a simple account of a mother's summer in France with three children. My manuscript skirted the dark crevasses essential to a life story. But I was learning the discipline of writing and perseverance.

After visits to several Junipero Serra missions with adobe architecture, I felt an echo of my beloved Europe and signed up for beginning Spanish at the local community center.

Sitting next to me in class was Nadia. She had curly blond hair, an overbite and manic energy. Sentences spun out of her mouth in a frenzy that initiated or deterred friendships. A transplant from the East Coast, she joked, "I don't talk fast, you listen slow," as I became her cautious new buddy. Nadia wanted to study Spanish with me between classes. Soon I was flooded with her fervor for Edgar Cayce, a mystic who could cure people a continent away by going into a trance. I visited her ranch house where her lunging Great Dane rose on hind feet to paw my shoulders. As she pulled at his collar, she thumbed through the latest Cayce volume looking for a particular passage to sway me.

Without actually saying, "Can't we go home?" our three daughters were mourning. I decided a little pet might help. We chose a hamster over a mouse or rat. Celeste was enchanted. She hurried home after school to feed the potato-sized rodent and watch him spin the exercise wheel. We could hear him whirring like a toy airplane working off angst at night. He had personality, vigor, nerve. One morning our youngest rushed in to greet her furry pet to find the cage empty. I heard a wailing.

"He's gone! He's not in his cage!" Sobbing followed.

We launched a search through the house. No hamster turned up. Gradually, the animal led us on such a chase that I conceived a children's story of a hamster's adventures. I titled it *I, Llewester* because we were watching *I, Claudius* on television at the time.

With the hamster manuscript typed and edited (and Llewester located,) I researched publishing houses. I still have a copy of my letter, sent to "Mrs. Anne P. Day, Dept. of Books for Boys and Girls, Harper and Row, Publishers." Dated February 11, 1967, the letter had two lines, showing I had sent an inquiry.

Dear Mrs. Day,

Enclosed is the manuscript, I, Llewester, for your consideration. Thank you for your letter.

Sincerely,
Julie H. Parker (Mrs. Peter Parker)

Temporary distraction resolved, I returned to my principal tale, the foreigner who went back to Europe with her three offspring. The manuscript absorbed me. Peter and our girls were in another world. I entered it long enough to tend to their basic requirements, then exited. The enchantment of our summer in France wooed me to the escapist world of the typewriter.

As I realized that returning to Illinois looked less likely, we received a letter from good friends from the Unitarian Church in Hinsdale. They were planning a spring business trip to Southern California. An enjoyable and attractive young couple with children the ages of ours, they asked if they might visit us.

"Is Christopher going to come too?" Diane brightened a moment. Their negative response depressed her.

This interim year, difficult for our girls despite trips to beaches and Knott's Berry Farm, was for Peter the launching of his own business career. He would soon step into full management of the California acquisition, outgrowing his old Chicago position as assistant engineer.

Two months had now elapsed with no response from Harper & Row. This pleased me, assuming the longer the silence, the more likely a positive response. I envisioned only two possible outcomes: acceptance or rejection, with no gray area of in-betweens. I recited to myself my story's opening, sure to impress an editor: "*There are cats and dogs and rats and frogs and once there were hogs up at Woofenpeeper's Pet Shop. But none is as clever as I, Llewester . . .*"

Our Hinsdale friends arrived, bringing fond memories of dinners together and mild crisscrossing attractions. Abby looked stunning. She was witty, observant, chatty. Her lovely presence in our home while her husband attended meetings pulled me out of my writing mode. Flirting and laughing, she charmed all of us, in particular, Peter. Suddenly I became aware that my preoccupation with the manuscript had been leaving my dear mate in a vacuum. My antennae flew up watching Peter and Abby banter as their glances lingered on each other.

"So you're leaving your old friends for this new barren land of California?"

"Oh, now that you're reminding us of what good times we all had together, I'm not so sure!" Peter was enjoying this playful attention.

"Oh nonsense . . . you know the ocean and mountains are making poor old Hinsdale seem like the flats!"

"Hinsdale had the greatest friends on earth . . . we don't know a soul here in Whittier!"

"I don't believe a minute of it . . . Julie says you're in the process of buying an old Spanish hacienda! We are dying to see it!"

Abby teased and Peter laughed a little too spontaneously.

As I observed our Hinsdale friend with my husband, something inside shrank a little. A wave of moroseness settled in, and with it guilt. I felt dull compared to Abby, who radiated vivacity. A self-condemning dialogue began. *"My head and heart aren't here in this world anymore. They are there . . . in the notebook, on the typewriter, climbing word by word into 'authorship.' I've let the most important person in my life, my support, my true love, slip into Abby's fingers."*

The next day, affirming Jung's theory of synchronicity, a letter arrived with the mail marked *Harper and Row, Publishers* in its upper left corner. Abby happened to be present. Both Peter and her husband had driven off to their separate work-related appointments. I pried open the envelope flap uncertainly. It was a short message, two sentences:

"Dear Mrs. Parker,

We have spent some time discussing your manuscript, I, Llewester, and have decided against publishing it. We would, however, like to see more of your work.

Sincerely, . . . "[7]

---

7. I have lost that letter, and recall only that it was short, containing the rejection, and the request to see more work. As I remember, there was also an indication that the decision to reject publication had taken time.

Shocked, I burst into tears. Abby, to whom I had confided hopes for my two manuscripts, tried to soothe me.

"Maybe another publisher will respond positively. Harper's is, after all, your first attempt. You mustn't be discouraged." She put her arm around me.

I was inconsolable. My ego had just experienced a double collapse, one part of which I could hardly share with Abby. I was unable to see the tremendous compliment the letter contained, and the encouragement to write more. I could have developed Llewester into a protagonist of many dimensions, cunning, quick-witted, yet bound to lose. Harper's must have recognized the character's possibilities. When Abby read the manuscript, she suggested I give Llewester a redeeming trait or two ... could I find a way to have him bond with the girls, become a little more endearing, like Ratty in *The Wind in The Willows?* My deflation was too pervasive. I was about to let Harper's down, Llewester down, and my own career as a writer. And I was about to discover how far I was from healed.

18

Crevasse

Abby was right. We had made an offer on a house that looked straight out of Moorish Spain. We had been warned to avoid Pasadena where smog settled in at the foot of the San Gabriel Mountains and schools were in turmoil over a court order mandating desegregation. But Pasadena had architectural integrity. Homes we could afford in cities near the ocean crowded against one another with tasteless facades, overwhelming the lots they sat upon. The only neighborhoods with spreading lawns in generous proportion to living space were those of the Pasadena area.

Our rustic hacienda of muslin-colored stucco was actually in unincorporated Altadena pressing tightly against the San Gabriel Mountains with roaming bobcats, bears, and an occasional mountain lion. It had a marvelous ornamental balcony, an authentic roof of overlapping molded red tiles, and a brick-floored entryway featuring a curling ornamental iron banister and stairway. Over the massive living room arched a heavy beamed cathedral ceiling. Doors on either side of a giant picture window led out to a back patio supported by rough-hewn wooden uprights. The spacious walled lawn beyond included a garden shed in one corner where Peter could do woodwork and store tools.

Although the current owners had carpeted all the floors the color of haze and painted every closet door to match the gray walls, even hanging heavy draperies across every glass opening, I imagined ways to make the home breathable like that of Peter's family. It needed polished bare floors, Persian rugs and paint removal to expose the beautiful oak doors and woodwork. It begged for art, for copper accents and curtainless views of the greenery outside.

The Pasadena area was in a massive slump caused by white flight, making home prices affordable. Desegregation, so abhorrent to many parents, was an experiment in equity and diversity that attracted me. Peter was less sure. But we now had a fine view of Mount Wilson of early telescope fame and were five minutes from mountain trails to a campground. We had signed papers making the house our own just before the arrival of our friends Abby and her husband.

Suddenly, with the double deflation of a manuscript rejected and Abby outshining my usual vivacity, I feared this move. California turned intimidating. For the first time since recovery eight years earlier, my confidence faltered. I wandered aimlessly in the rented house worrying about what Peter and the children might think. My hand on the tiller had slipped; the wind in my sail, that joyous billowing tugging the family forward in all-consuming projects, had stilled. In the unexpected vacuum I sank into depression. As rapidly as the onset of earlier episodes, my self-assurance spun into dread and the fickle mirror of my image twisted against itself. Could mental illness be resurfacing? Would I be sent back to an asylum?

Peter, now habituated to my absorption in activities that gave him freedom to define his own passions and develop his growing leadership potential, was blindsided by my sudden unmooring. It was a time of tension for him; he needed my stability. His Los Angeles business was tackling project development in the field of massive hydraulic lifting equipment. In several years, his company would be hired to do the jacking of the 800-ton center span of the Fremont Bridge crossing the Willamette River in Portland, Oregon. It was a hoisting project whose scale would cause any manager to have nightmares of the center section crashing into the river below.

This was a pivotal moment, again, when I hovered, not between two continents on an ocean liner, but between two vastly different metropoles. We were giving up the comfortable little suburb Hinsdale near the Midwest's proudly solid Chicago for a town in the rootless shadow of edgy Los Angeles. I hadn't thought of the hospital experience in years, but now those terrible times surfaced as almost heroic in memory, my determination and Peter's devotion helping me regain health—almost too much health. My vigor for writing, for foreign travel, for languages and embracing causes had added a new one: desegregation. The girls were used to me dashing from room to room, talking excitedly, smiling at anything catching my amusement, especially aural quirks like Katherine complaining her teacher was a "grosh."

Now I hung my head, forehead muscles drawn, mouth corners sagging, and sank into a poisonous pit of fear and shame. Was this depression? If so, depression was far less deadly than psychosis, but it had its own disabling grip upon me. Psychosis was dramatic. It sent one to an asylum. Depression let me loiter about home in embarrassment, provoking family disrespect rather than empathy.

Crawling into bed the minute the family left for school and work, I felt helpless in this not quite mentally ill state, disgusted by my whimpering cowardice. Shame kept me from sharing feelings with Peter.

With such energy desertion my hair grew dirtier and ungroomed, my clothes sagged and smelled. And I now froze over a new possibility: Peter might tire of me. I vacillated between panic at that possibility and thoughts of life's meaninglessness. Why should I struggle if the old enemy kept resurfacing, a sadistic foe wiping out each temporary triumph? Like a burning city's toxic ash, hopelessness sifted in.

Peter, in contrast, was exhilarated by the Pacific and Sierras.

"I know this move feels tough, but let's pull together," he coaxed. "Our new home needs us to paint, furnish and plan the garden as a team. You're great at gardens. We're in a Shangri-la, Julie, bordered by ocean, desert and the San Gabriel mountain range!"

I moped. "But you're all wrapped up in your new business life and planning a climb up Mt. Whitney with your work buddies. I'm happy for you; I just hate this terrible feeling."

Peter loved California's topography as I loved France's. Shrinking with guilt, I tucked *I, Llewester* into a drawer. Suddenly, nothing was firm or reassuring. A month before moving in, when for the first time we drove our three girls past the rustic two-story with its iron grillwork protecting windows, Katherine scowled.

"It looks like a jail."

"Aren't we ever going to go back to Hinsdale again?"

Diane's sadness mirrored my own uprootedness.

"We'll go back to visit as often as we want." I tried to cheer myself for the sake of our daughters.

My letters to quiet, lovely Louise had been full of the thrill of writing projects. Now, with a choke in my larynx, I poured out lines of loneliness. I watched the mail for her responses. At the same time I continued weekly Spanish lessons. Nadia, as talkative as ever, noticed something different in her companion. She pried a little. I shared only that my story had been rejected. She was mystified by why this was causing such a change in me. I skipped two sessions to avoid her searching questions.

It was on a May evening, particularly still outside except for a lone mockingbird singing for his unseen female. A quiet breeze wafted now and then through the screened front door of our rental. The children were stealing glances at one another through the strain at the dinner table as I stared into a void. The five of us were eating scalloped potatoes and meatloaf that I had spent extra time preparing, in a forced display of responsibility as a wife and mother. Suddenly, rising up from my chair to bring in second helpings, I staggered slightly, then without warning, my entire frame crumpled and collapsed onto the carpet.

"Mama!" cried Diane in alarm as Katherine burst into tears. Peter rushed to me on the floor and bent over, calling loudly "Julie? Julie?" There was no response.

"Stay here girls, while I get the car started. We're going to rush Mama to the hospital!"

Peter dashed out and within two minutes came running back through the front door. With Diane's help, the two carried me, dead to all appearances, out into the rear compartment of the red square-back Volkswagen we had picked up at the dock of the Port of Los Angeles. All three sisters climbed in a panic into seats back and front next to their father. He drove the car directly to the regional Whittier Hospital, around the Whitwood Shopping Center, pulling the car into the Emergency Department entrance. Soon the hospital staff had wheeled me into a treatment room where several nurses and an intern took vital signs. Diane, Katherine and Celeste waited in a lounge area with their father. He held his girls in his arms, trying to comfort them.

I remember that trip, curled into the back section of our Volkswagen as if it were yesterday. During that ten-minute ride I was having a near-death experience, a psychic one. Reviewing my thirty-five years of life I felt a deep calm, tallying the ages of each daughter and making peace with what I had done for them as their mother. It was a self-evaluation, matter-of-fact. Though it felt too bad to die young, I had done my best and was no longer guilt-ridden or morose. I had been treated for a small ulcer two weeks earlier. The sense of a sudden whoosh accompanying my collapsing could only mean one thing—my ulcer was bleeding. I was dying. Next, I remember seeing myself from above on an examining table in the emergency room looking down, surrounded by puzzled faces. My lips must have moved.

"Why are you whispering?" one of the nurses asked me. I sighed, barely audible.

"Because I am bleeding to death."

"No you're not," came the answer. "Your vital signs are all normal. We can't find anything wrong with you."

As I heard this jarring assessment from a consciousness floating overhead, I emerged from that altered state; normal intelligence clicked back in. Something was amiss. The nurses' reassurance shocked whatever out-of-body experience had taken hold of me. As it dissipated, I began to feel my ordinary awareness slowly replace the strange space it had been in, overhead. But no medical explanation covered this odd spell.

What had happened was a variation upon inexplicable episodes from the past, first as an eight-year-old screaming, "I'm dying." Like one coming out of a coma, I felt estranged, confused, and shaken.

The nurses helped me back onto my feet and led me into the office of the doctor on call, Dr. Queensberry. Peter was summoned in from the waiting area where he had been comforting the girls. Together we heard the doctor speak to my husband.

"Your wife has had an abnormal experience. I suggest you find psychological help for her as soon as possible."

Bewildered, I had to agree with the physician. Indeed, it was abnormal. It seemed, however, that what had just happened should be more accurately defined as *beyond* normal. I had fainted before, initiating psychosis. Fainters lose the power of awareness along with consciousness. They "come to" surprised, wondering what happened or why they are on the floor. I, to the contrary, had experienced a state quite different, stepping out of the parameters of earthbound time to enter a telescopic spying upon my life's contributions. From that strange vantage point, I summarized accomplishments up to that point with a calmness that shed deep peace. All the way home in the car, now sitting next to Peter while the girls remained traumatized in the back seat, I tried to make sense of this strange occurrence. It caused a consciousness dissonance. My ordinary mindset had temporarily been usurped by a strange, altered state.

Back at Spanish class Nadia, the only Whittier friend with whom I could share a little of the baffling incident, continued prying. She was fascinated by my strange episode. It launched a barrage of theories linked to her studies exploring reincarnation. They were all too hare-brained, especially spewing forth from a woman whose obsessiveness made me draw back.

"Julie, you have got to consider Edgar Cayce, the Sleeping Prophet! He had out-of-body experiences daily."

"Nadia, I'm not interested in that kind of thing. It is too bizarre."

"But Julie, Cayce's books can help you understand what just happened to you. Cayce was this amazing psychic who healed people miles away. You have got to write to The Cayce Foundation and get a reading."

I brushed off Nadia's ranting and felt a new distaste for conversing with her.

A mood change, however, had definitely set in for all of us. The familiar lush green lawns of our Midwest neighborhood memories were receding before our current surroundings of crabgrass clumps clawing desert sand. Each of us handled our relocating in solitude. Our daughters were left without their cheery mother's reassurance at a time that was critical in their development. For six years my confidence had grown in Illinois, supporting the children emotionally. Now everything predictable in our family life was crumbling. Diane's identity was tied to her tomboy club friends in Illinois at age eleven. On the cusp of puberty, she would have been challenged even without a transfer to California. The timing of this move was particularly hard on the sisters. Their mother appeared to be decomposing once again.

By the end of the Whittier school year we had sold our dear, white picket fenced home on York Road and met the movers as they delivered our furniture to our Spanish home. We felt sober. There was a spreading jacaranda tree on the front lawn whose lavender blooms burst forth in May. Diane chose the front bedroom that looked out upon its graceful lacy leaves and the street over a decorative bit of ironwork at the base of her window. Katherine picked a large room next to ours on the back of the house, and Celeste ended up with the most interesting one with its own little corner fireplace and double French doors opening upon a wraparound balcony.

At Peter's urging I had followed Dr. Queensberry's advice to set up an appointment with a new psychiatrist, Dr. Hartwell. He asked me if I had ever heard of Zen. I had not. He gave me a list of ten aphorisms that encouraged detachment and enjoyment of small things, "gathering the flowers along the way," "so what, I'll do." I continued for five or six visits. He described me as a "chair with three strong legs and one gimpy one."

At Spanish class for the next to last session, Nadia asked how I was doing. She expressed dubiousness about conventional therapy.

"Julie, you just *have* to read this book by Edgar Cayce, *Beyond Death . . . Visions of the Other Side.*" I have another one too by Joan Grant, *Many Lifetimes . . .* "

"Nadia, stop." My objection was drowned by her urgency.

"It will explain what you have just experienced, and give you guidance." Her rush of words now scared me.

"Nadia, I don't want to hear any more about these odd theories. I have no interest in any ideas like reincarnation. Please stop talking about it."

A few days later at our final Spanish class together she was juggling three books.

"Julie, I want you just to take a glance at one book by Cayce. Or let me read a little to you. Cayce is healing people he doesn't even know, across the country from him. He is amazing!

"Nadia, please . . ."

"No, Julie . . . you really need to consider the idea of reincarnation. He tells people about their past lives, and it helps explain so much to them. It might explain the experience you have just gone through."

With her words shooting like bullets at her listeners, Nadia was wearing me to the point of fracture. As she started in again, I snapped.

"Nadia, if you don't stop talking about Edgar Cayce I can't continue to see you. You're scaring me with your constant talk about this guy who doesn't appeal to me. I come from a family of doctors, you know. I'm very depressed. I'm sorry, Nadia."

I spoke in a hurtful voice; it seemed the only way to stem her bombardment.

Nadia withdrew a little. I had indeed injured her. She responded quietly, and for the first time, in measured words, showed deep feeling.

"Then all right. I value your friendship. The only thing that seems curious about your objection is that reincarnation is for me such a reassuring theory." She was not her usual self as she reflected. She was pensive, appealing.

"For me," she said quietly, "it is very comforting to think that perhaps we have lived before and perhaps we will live again. It is such a generous idea . . . that everyone will have life after life to progress toward fulfillment. Even in the Bible there are references to it. Even . . ." She trailed off, realizing she was right back on the offending turf.

I went home to our little rental on Portada Drive that we were emptying of scattered papers, books and toys. Everything was sad. Even Llewester, whom we had found drowned in our pool, now symbolized end times. The memory of our children's grief that morning, finding him floating motionless in the chlorinated water, bespoke lives and deaths passing vainly. He had escaped captivity and surely struggled; none of us had been awake to rescue him from the slippery tiled edge.

That night I lay in bed thinking about Nadia and her last remark. Her fixation was weird, but so were certain of my unexplainable episodes. For the first time, I looked at my own thirty-five years of life and its unusual eruptions. They bewildered physicians. There was something "unscientific" in my experiences, beginning in childhood at age eight. Strange episodes left parents, doctors, even friends baffled. I kept dying with no physical cause. And how odd it was to hear a psychic pronounce to me, a student in Paris, that I had "died young," presumably in a former existence. What was causing all this deceptive death drama while being in sound physical health? The enigma was about to turn life upside down for Peter and me.

19

Trompe l'oeil

"Sometimes I feel as if a demon is plaguing us. Just as everything begins to go smoothly, you have a setback." Peter whammed the mattress in frustration. His fist narrowly missed my jaw.

"I know. I feel it too," I whispered helplessly, pathetically.

My husband's discouragement was almost more frightening than mine. Sitting motionless in the living room, autumn torpor on the faithful pine sofa bed in the late afternoon, I saw my mind getting sucked into the old danger zone. The fear came and went. I knew, rationally, that I needed to take firm hold in our new home. Instead, I mounted the brick stairway and lay down on our bed upstairs, pulling a quilt over my knees. I hugged my chest as tears flowed. What Peter saw when he returned from work looked like weak-willed sulking, an individual dragging him into the painful past.

One Sunday we decided to attend the local Unitarian church to see if it might help us feel more anchored in our community. At the coffee hour we gravitated toward an attractive Latino couple standing a little apart with their twin daughters about Katherine's age. We introduced ourselves as newcomers and the two responded with charming accents that they were here on a year's sabbatical for Roberto, an artist in

Guadalajara. His wife Mariana was helping fill out his meager stipend by offering Spanish classes. Roberto, throwing his head back to shake his wild black hair out of his eyes, was typically macho, talking non-stop about his position at the *instituto* back home and thriving painting career. He fixated on me somewhat, winking and joking as I tried out my limited Spanish to his encouragement. Our girls talked with the twins who giggled as they struggled to use their new English words. Mariana, who was a slim beauty with dark shining hair and deep soulful eyes, smiled at Peter gently while her husband dominated in a way she ignored. I could see Peter was quite taken with her. By the end of the social hour Roberto insisted we come visit their rented home to see his studio. Mariana interested me much more than Roberto. I asked her if she might consider giving me private Spanish lessons. She responded enthusiastically. It was arranged that she would come to our home weekly.

At our first lesson Mariana, lonely during this novel year, seemed almost over-eager to bond with our family. She wanted to see our home both downstairs and up. Her warmth and situation similar to my own as a newcomer encouraged me to share my insecurity a little about living in California. This touched her on levels I was not aware of.

One day while Peter was at work, I had an idea, morose over the gloomy gray living room rug underfoot and sagging draperies. Mariana had arrived early for our lesson. I pulled up one corner of the carpeting. It separated rather easily from the fir-stripping full of nail points all around the giant room's perimeter. Soon my new friend was helping me tug and pull. We called a handyman. Within an hour the next day, the entire carpet had been detached, rolled up and hauled out onto the front lawn. A dark floor made up of thin hardwood planks in perfect condition gave me a sudden lift. It was a first step to recreating Peter's family's lovely oak floors.

Mariana lingered after our lesson, in no hurry to return to Roberto's bidding. She enjoyed partnering with me as if sharing a little of our spousal life vicariously. The huge cathedral-ceilinged room intimidated me. She thought a Roberto painting might increase hominess. The giant fireplace at one end looked straight out of the great hall in Sigrid Undset's medieval saga *Kristin Lavransdatter*. I waffled, not drawn to anything "Roberto." There was too much eagerness in Mariana, as if her fervor were nudging mine aside.

One Friday we responded to Mariana's invitation to see Roberto's studio and share tapas with them. Meeting Roberto for the second time gave a clear picture of his relationship with his wife, who played a Vermeer pearl-earring-girl role to her husband. They had rented a small house with a large workshop behind it. As he strutted about this studio, proudly pointing out the works an art gallery was interested in, Mariana followed unenthused, describing her duties putting away paint tubes at the end of the day, cleaning brushes and organizing his wild output of abstract works drying on every surface. His canvases made me uncomfortable . . . garish red pillars lined against greenish trompe l'oeil columns almost felt like an artist's trap. Roberto gestured and tapped my shoulder, his eyes seeking mine for approval. This unsought attention left Mariana free to chat with Peter. They laughed and joked together, as he had joked with Abby in Whittier. The more playful Peter was with Mariana, the more nervous I became. This affected our relationship during our Spanish lessons. My role as one impaired became a little more pronounced while hers as caregiver-teacher expanded. She bounced into our home as if sprung from tedium.

"*Julia? Te sientes mejor hoy, querida amiga? Te he traído unas naranjas de nuestro arbol. Deje me hacer jugo para ti . . . donde está tu exprimidor de naranja?*"

I did not feel comfortable with Mariana bringing me oranges and asking where the squeezer was to make juice in my kitchen. Dampening her cheer felt mean-spirited. Spanish lessons were helping to distract me somewhat from depression. But Mariana's tutoring gave her a certain command of our situation. One day, when I felt especially discouraged, she made a suggestion.

"*Julia, tu estás cansada.* Here, let us go *arriba*, upstairs. Why don't you lie down a while." Pronouncing me tired, she took my arm surprisingly authoritatively. She puffed at our bed pillows and smoothed the covers motheringly. Something felt cautionary. She was in our bedroom, Peter's and mine!

Accustomed in my youth to being the one with the charisma while Mother often sulked, I was not used to being out-charmed. Mariana left an upbeat breeze behind her and though she never mentioned him, I intuited that she had a crush on my husband. All she ever said was in reference to Roberto, whom she pouted over.

"*Que suerte que tu tienes, Julia. Roberto me traita como su criada. Tu esposo es generoso, y tan atento con tigo.*"

I didn't care if Roberto treated her like a maid! I did not need her telling me Peter was generous and attentive! We continued meeting them at church; Peter especially enjoyed the social hours. Mariana always appeared coquettish in dresses with ruffles at the sleeves or a revealing peekaboo neckline. I felt obligated to have the four of them come to our home for drinks.

They arrived on a lovely warm evening. While the girls played outside with the twins in the backyard, Roberto roamed around our living room pointing out places one of his paintings would offer a perfect accent. He asked Mariana to go out to the car to bring in a couple canvases he happened to have previewed to a curator that day. She appeared, lugging in two awkward frames with annoyance. Roberto rushed forth to set them down, reprimanding, '*Cuidado, mujer!*' then grabbed her and gave her a forceful smooch that she steeled against. He laughed as he grinned at me and winked.

"Mariana and I are explosive."

Mariana almost too quickly followed Peter out to the kitchen where I had plates of hors d'oeuvre partly ready, and wine glasses on a tray waiting for a bottle of chardonnay chilling in the refrigerator. I was trapped in the living room by Roberto, who was trying to get either a sale or a little attraction going between us. He walked around with the pictures, holding them up on various wall spaces, pinning my presence at each step by questions.

"*Que piensas? Aqui, o mejor aqui?*"

I couldn't concentrate or care where his art would look best, hearing Peter and Marianna laughing in the kitchen. Was Roberto aware that his wife and my husband were engaged in a playful flirtation? I finally broke away, and found them by the sink, Peter with the wine bottle in hand, Mariana a little too close, watching as he extricated the cork easily. Had anything transpired between them? Had I imagined an embarrassed little pulling back, a surprised turn toward me upon my kitchen entry? The children's plate of sandwiches and cookies had not been carried out to them; the adult plate of cheeses and olives, shrimp and crackers sat where I had set it. Mariana had done nothing; there sat the other tray, empty, next to napkins, knives, small plates, two sauces. Almost guiltily she now asked how she could help bring everything into the living room. I asked her to take snacks out into the yard to set on a folding table for the children. Roberto sat on our sofa with his legs outstretched.

"We four should all go out to the desert together someday. I know a little inn that isn't too expensive. We could have a ball."

Roberto was in his element. I tightened up immediately at such an idea but noticed Mariana and my husband glance at each other. I remained silent, feeling like a killjoy. Peter chimed in, inquiring whether the place might be near Joshua Tree, a park he wanted us to visit. We had now known the couple for two months. Despite trying to decorate various rooms and continue progressing in Spanish, I feared my depression was worsening. When our new Mexican friends left, I felt melancholic. Witnessing my husband so light-hearted around Mariana made me feel like a sack, stone-weighted.

For the next month I moved between fear over the persistent depression and guilt over failing my family. The pattern appeared to be gaining. The recurring thought, *Why struggle*, terrified me by what it signified—losing everything in life I held precious. These obsessive words were so debilitating that I kept returning to my bed after helping the girls make lunch sandwiches and seeing them off to school with a pale smile.

The next day I felt something so desperate menacing survival that it compelled me to act. I struck out from our home and walked down the street in a daze. I sought a human being, any human being other than Mariana. I had met two families briefly in addition to elderly next-door neighbors. Ghostlike, I knocked on the front door of one. The woman called out that she was on the phone and to come back another time. Continuing a little further I crossed the street and rang, knocking on a second door. I had met May walking her dog but couldn't remember her first name. "Gay?" I asked, when she answered the bell. She looked puzzled, then corrected me, "I'm May." I blurted out, "I'm sorry, but I am desperate. I need to be near someone." Perhaps I added "I think I'm dying."

May did something comforting. She invited me in and suggested I lie down and rest in her college daughter's bedroom. I probably looked faint. She brought me a glass of water or tea, I don't remember. She offered a mother's empathy. After an hour or two of resting on the top of that bed with a small quilt May had spread over me, I thanked her and went home. It created a little bond.

But an hour later panic set in. When Peter returned from work that night, I explained what had happened. Looking down at myself, I realized my brown pants were wrinkled, a loose checkered shirt hung limply, missing a button, and my stringy hair accentuated hollows under my eyes. I looked at him, pleading. He shook his head in puzzlement. When Celeste called for homework help, he left me in the kitchen without a word.

The next afternoon, a sense of finality set in. I had sunk into a perilous crater. That was it. There was no way out. The battle for my health was over. I surrendered. Why had I not seen it before? Why was I uselessly torturing myself, when symptoms would always return and win in the end? I felt a deep peace, a dying of the struggle. What felt best was that I had not shirked my duty; I had tried everything humanly possible. It was, at last, finality. In a way it was a variation of what had happened three months earlier in Whittier, en route to the nearest hospital. But this was a conscious act.

In a sense of momentous succumbing, I sought a physical place in our downstairs to lay my head and body down to complete the rite of giving up. For some reason I chose the small loveseat, new, in Peter's den. I stretched out, symbolically seeing myself yielding life. There was a vague picture in my mind's eye that when Peter came home, he would find me there, then order the insane asylum attendants to come and take me away. I saw them in their white coats, bearing me on a stretcher, almost hymn-like, *comin' for to carry me home.*

What happened next was thunderous. In a bolt from another dimension, a Voice spoke from within me shouting, "Good God, Julie. What is the matter with you! Do you realize you have the power of God inside you! Power of the Almighty!! You are amazing! Do you think you could have endured all this so far without that power? What ails you, woman!! Get up off that bed and take hold of your power! Get up right this minute!"

Stunned, I rose like Lazarus. I had just undergone a rebirth of some sort. My little shrinking self suddenly felt imbued with an enormous strength. It was thrilling, life-affirming!

The old extrovert impulse to share everything, to reach out rather than withdraw, drove what I did next. I got into the car and headed straight to Mariana and Roberto's house, full of this Voice. I must have looked wild-eyed. Roberto met me at the door.

"*Que pasa*, Julia?"

"Roberto, I have just been struck with an amazing insight!"

In the hallway, I started sharing what had just happened incoherently. But it was as if scales had peeled from my eyes. I was explaining.

"Roberto, do you see what is happening? Do you know our partners really like each other, and that it is okay ... everything is okay ... and we all are going to be fine!!" Mariana heard me ranting and came running into the living room in her own panic.

The next scene could be described, again, as out of Jungian synchronicity. Mariana started shouting, "Has Peter said anything? Has Peter called you? What are you talking about! What has just happened? What has Peter said? Have you just gotten some kind of a phone call?" Then she lost her self-control and screamed, "Has Peter betrayed us?"

I was stunned. But not Roberto. He stared at his wife witheringly and said, "Not Again, Mariana ... oh, no, not again ... "

Mariana now came unglued. She began to beat at her husband's shoulders and chest, fists clenched, screeching, "I hate you! I hate you!" Roberto turned to me and said, "You can see my wife is not well. Do you see? If she has something going on with Peter, it won't be the first time. This is her pattern. Mariana is a two-faced woman."

As he spoke, she clawed at him and scared me with her violence. She was seething with revulsion for her husband. "I may cook for you and clean your studio but you will never possess my heart! Never!" Her voice took on a tone I had only witnessed in the psychiatric hospital, or in my own hallucinations, cunning, destructive.

It now became clear that more had been going on between Mariana and Peter than either Roberto or I realized. I left the two of them,

Mariana struggling, Roberto restraining, and headed home awakened to a new turn of events. Within an hour Peter would be returning. In the interim, however, either Roberto had ordered her, or Mariana on her own initiative had called Peter at his office. It turned out she knew his number there well.

What puzzles me as I remember the next scenes is the absence of our daughters. Yet I remember clearly conversing with Peter in his den. Perhaps the girls had been sent over to the school playground around the corner to drum up a game. Diane was the ace of tetherball and neighborhood kids hung around until dinnertime. At any rate, I had found a way to ensure a period of privacy to confront Peter. He drove into the garage; I was waiting for him.

"So, you have been secretly meeting and having phone conversations with Mariana at work?"

"Yes, I have. I am in love with Mariana." This remark framed our situation, a ménage à trois.

"Can you describe just what has been going on?"

"Nothing much has been going on, except meeting a few times. And phone calls at work."

"Tell me about these meetings."

"Once we met at the Huntington Hotel."

"And what happened there? Have you two had sex together?"

"No, we have not. We kissed a lot. I promised her a silver necklace."

"Well, have you figured out what you want to do with your future? Do you want a divorce?"

"No, I have thought about that, and I do not plan to divorce, for the sake of the children." His remark was histrionic, so stock it was comical.

"This is ridiculous! You have simply lost your head temporarily!"

"Well, that may be. It is for sure you have not been much of a partner recently. In fact Mariana is hard-working, trying to be a support at home to Roberto. You seem like an old shoe. Dragging, depressed. It has felt pretty hopeless at times. You just haven't been there for any of us."

Peter was right. But this sudden change triggered a streak of common sense from my turmoil. After all, I had just heard the Voice. "You know," I said in total control, "I believe this is a passing infatuation. I believe you will come to your senses. If you had seen Mariana this afternoon the way I saw her, I think you would recognize she is not the person she may seem to you. I think you'll want to talk to Roberto."

"Maybe so. But right now my heart is not with you. I feel sad and even guilty about it. But you have not helped much." Silently, I knew he spoke the truth. Symptoms had scrambled me into a deplorable facsimile of myself.

The next day Peter and Roberto met at a café. Peter learned from him perplexing truths about Mariana, the main one being that she had a pattern of infidelity. Guadalajara was sprinkled with cast-off lovers. The guilty reconciliations, Roberto confided to Peter, were the most treasured moments of their marriage. The artist did not realize the role he played in fostering these infatuations. Roberto was enslaved to Mariana's charms and knew that basically she did not respect or love him. Peter came home from the visit deflated. His feelings for the lovely Mexican were entangled with hers for him. He realized they must be teased apart, a trying period for the two of us.

This dénouement, however, was a blessing to our marriage like the slap that starts a baby breathing. The idea that Peter had illicitly fallen in love triggered a powerful new sensuality in me, setting me burning sexually. I had to confront an embarrassing truth: my libido was aroused by insecurity, by being spurned. I thought of my girlhood adoration of George, who had scorned me. The evidence that Peter, too, had frailties in our marriage boosted my ego. I was not the only one with failings. He was no longer the model of dependability and faithful supportiveness that had been so predictable it killed attraction.

Was something in me pushing him to misstep? I did not like that part of me, especially if it caused my own incapacitation. Were my "mental" symptoms simply masking a longing for Peter to threaten to desert me, to make me grow up?

The Daemon leans forward, showing unusual interest in this turn of events.

"Do you see how these blind behaviors, these slumps, have locked our protagonist in helplessness, Cerulea? Notice their cleverness, containing the keys that can spring open the cage of her will within . . . "

"And that powerful voice! It revealed her strength, waiting for a moment of surrender. I feel for her, Daemon. She is honest, blaming no one, moving forward little by little. Oh, how painful it is."

The Fairy inspects the veil for tears needing mending.

The power of my sudden attraction for my husband was proof that depression plays its own game. Humbly, I realized I was like all people who mess things up in bizarre ways to create opportunities to become fully mature human beings. I now grew alert to these patterns, these symptoms that surfaced every time our life faced a difficult passage. My illness was a form of addiction! From childhood, no one had ever helped me learn how to pitch in when the going got tough. Mother and various helpers did it all, either cheerfully, or in Mother's case, whiningly. But Mother *did* it. She cared for Celeste the year I broke down. I was disgusted with my symptoms, hiding parts of me I was not proud of.

As Peter tried to work through his broken heart, he shared things he had always excused but never admired about me.

"When I need help you are always somewhere else. You're always preoccupied with your own interests. I like your imaginativeness, but you and I are out of balance. I find myself resenting it."

He pointed out that I was self-absorbed. He felt taken for granted. I knew he was right. I wanted to overcome this selfishness.

The training started in little ways. One day, Peter had a huge pile of brush he had trimmed from our bushes and orange trees in the backyard. He called me to come out and help him cut the pile into short lengths to fit into our trash can. For the first time in my life I worked by his side. I bent over again and again gathering branches. It felt strange, not my work. Yet with each branch cut I felt a new pride, a new little refrain. "I am helping Peter. I am doing what I have never done before." I looked around for observers. This was new! I wanted the world to know I was doing something dull, humdrum, something I had feared, unawares, that it might make me whine like Mother, be consumed by Mother's dolefulness. Or maybe such dull tasks would bind me, stick me to the earth, unable to take flight into the infinite blue, the blue I had tried to clutch onto, that vast dreamy boundlessness I was leaving behind at my moment of birth.

Peter was a tough taskmaster. He now began to train me as his father had trained him, with unyielding scrutiny. I helped sweep up fall leaves.

"No, you've done a half-assed job. Look at all those you have left in the basement wells, and in that corner. Get those. Get every leaf!"

He pointed in irritation. He was a perfectionist like his parent. He had been trained to do a job right.

"How is this?"

"Fair. Look behind you . . . those bushes need to be raked out."

I tried to learn from him, but tended to be slap-bang. Slowly we became more of a team. Not a totally balanced one, but better. Small improvements made me feel proud.

"Look," I wanted him to see. "I have raked out every leaf the gardener blows into our azalea bushes. Now we can fertilize them. Now rain can get to them."

He smiled. We hugged and kissed and made love in thrilling passion that night.

I had never, even in the recent moments of Peter losing his head and heart temporarily, believed that anything could come between us permanently. Our love and commitment from the outset had been too layered with the uncanny, the beyond ordinary. To survive, perhaps our union needed to be slightly sullied, like the Persians weaving mistakes into their carpets so God wouldn't be jealous. But that commitment we had made, once we marveled at how we had found each other, seemed impervious to major dishonor. There was something profound—beyond human understanding—destined to survive all weakness and temptation. Even my "Voice" shouting out had an extraordinary timing to it, compelling me to go directly to Roberto and clear the air in the nick of time, before Peter could have succumbed to "the other woman." Had we two started out eons before, joined like a nautilus shell, then drifted apart? Had we always known each other and failed one another? Were we this time around meant to get it right, to complete one another? Nadia's idea of life before life seemed less unorthodox.

Gradually, Peter's feelings faded for the flawed and fluffy Mariana. He felt ashamed. He and I began to communicate more honestly with one another, and to address our shadow sides that had stumbled. We became more real to one another, a somewhat more balanced team. That church visit had initiated a baptism with its own momentum; there was no need to return to it. We never saw the Guadalajarans again. My depressed state lifted, but for the next two years I felt fragile, a disturbed perennial that was reluctant to root in non-native soil.

"Daemon, is that you chuckling?" Cerulea detects a slight jiggle.

"I grin now and then when protagonists emerge from the bellies of their own whales."

"So what do you predict will happen next?"

"Were you watching the agents of confrontation in this case . . . shame, escapism, guilt and insight?"

"Yes, of course. You forgot will. I'd say things look propitious." The Cerulean Fairy is ever optimistic.

The Daemon restrains a smile.

20

The Student is Ready, 1971

One day, feeling stronger but still at recurring moments like a wilted transplant, I remembered Yvette in Chicago. She had disappeared from French Club and reappeared a year later transformed by yoga. The word persisted because of its effect on her. Recalling also my veterinarian friend Philippe's fervor, I thought this odd form of exercise might help me. In the yellow pages there were three listings, one of which was in Pasadena, simply printed "Harvey Hansen, yoga instructor." The Beatles, too, inspired me with their holy man from India. Fans rushed to their guru, the Maharishi Mahesh Yogi, for initiation into his "TM," Transcendental Meditation. I dialed the phone number.

"Where do I come for your yoga?"

"I teach in my own home near Mountain Avenue."

"And who else will be there?"

"Just you and me. I see my students individually."

"And how do I know I am safe with you, a person I know nothing about?" I posed the question rather boldly.

"When you see me put a red feather in my cap, you'll know to be on your guard," he joked. This Mr. Hansen sounded older, quick-witted, nearby and perhaps holder of a key to something helpful.

Within a week I found my way to his tiny home on a cul-de-sac. I was ready to experiment with something on the fringe. The house sat back behind bushes. In the new black leotard he had told me to wear, I parked, slid out of the driver's seat, put on my raincoat and locked the car door. The neighborhood looked iffy.

Harvey met me at the door smiling, white-haired, tan-faced, perhaps in his late sixties. With a pleasant gravelly voice, limping a little, he showed where students took off their shoes and where I was to leave my towel later on a chair among a stack of others. His miniature living room was dark and full of artifacts from India: rugs, Buddha statues, wall hangings, a tiger skin. Joking that he was the "only Danish guru he knew of," he led me into a kind of inner sanctum, once a dining area, with his own small chair next to a queen-sized, flat, hard-surfaced platform raised off the floor. Harvey was relaxed, not self-absorbed. He directed me to sit upon the platform first while he would share a little introductory talk each time. His theories, totally new to me, focused upon the value of "Prana." He asked me to follow as he demonstrated deep, rhythmic, slow inhalations that seemed to alter his gaze slightly. His chest rose and sank visibly. I had a flashback to Philippe in Paris doing special breathing exercises in 1952.

Harvey next asked me to stand in the middle of the leather-covered platform, on my towel, to follow his instructions in a set of Hatha Yoga postures. He held a paper with a list of these moves on it, each one illustrated to help his students remember them at home. He selected an elementary set, beginning with a group of standing movements, that he directed me through slowly and carefully. They were easy to execute. As I moved, he watched carefully.

'Yes, just right. That is it, that's the way, hands outstretched, a little higher . . ."

He then led me into a group of slow movements of my upper torso, bending from the waist down, circling my chest area left and right. The postures were mostly stationary, enjoyable, calming, nothing like a dance or language class where the point is exactitude. Harvey reminded me to breathe deeply as I moved.

"Don't overstretch, keep peaceful, there is no hurry here, no perfect way. Yoga is about breathing in the energy of life, about calming oneself deep at the center, about letting go of stress."

As his voice soothed, I found the movements were revealing a lifelong tightness stringing my musculature together. The calm of his words, emphasizing there was no right or wrong way, slipped through my defensiveness. The experience tapped into a zone of serenity I did not know existed. Before the hour was up my new teacher had prompted me through a series of standing, sitting, back and abdomen stretches with words that whispered, "Cool it. Stop the fight for survival." Breathing slowly, I entered momentarily a tranquil state of effortlessness.

"All right. That is enough for today."

Harvey's voice brought me back to his humble domicile. I had entered it hesitantly, a cave of ambiguity, and now exited as an altered initiate. I returned to my parked car and drove home with a printout of postures illustrated with stick figures.

Peter and the girls were waiting for a report. They sensed something atypical in the way I floated through the door. I smiled secretively, saying I had done a new kind of stretching.

"But what is it like?" Diane wanted to know. "What's so special about bending?"

Outside she did a cartwheel on the lawn, then walked on her hands in perfect balance.

"It's unlike anything I've ever experienced before." I tried to share what was hard to describe.

"Show us that paper with the pictures on it. I want to see what's so great about it."

Diane scrutinized the little stick figures. They conveyed nothing of interest to her.

Over the next weeks, Harvey Hansen gave extensive explanations of the principles of yoga arising from Hinduism and the concept of karma. I absorbed the idea that human beings need to work through lower desires and ego stages before attaining a higher level of consciousness. The theory dovetailed, or at least did not fight with Western psychology's concept of the subconscious teaming with complexes that obstruct happiness. Harvey made me laugh. He never played guru, loftily spouting esoteric theories. I was the ready student, Harvey simply the unassuming teacher that had appeared.

As yoga became part of my regular practice, Peter's Unitarianism reacted.

"Who is this Harvey person? Do you know anything about his background?"

"Not much, Peter. But I'm not too worried about that. I'm experiencing a whole new way of looking at life. I'm feeling better, more peaceful."

"But is he legitimate? What is his training?" My husband wanted credentials. For the first time, our philosophical paths were diverging, mine taking me beyond academic skepticism.[8]

"I'm pretty savvy. I think I'll know if I sense something fake."

Peter, on unfamiliar ground, glanced at me dubiously.

Since the rejection of the *I, Llewester* manuscript, I had picked up the pace of corresponding with Louise, who was still in Illinois. Her letters had offered comfort when I inquired whether she had had relapses after her hospital stay. Not relapses, she had responded, so much as a continuous struggle with Bob's cavalier treatment of her as invisible. I felt discomfort. Perhaps Peter, like Louise, felt unseen.

Louise was my teacher without her realizing it. My latest letter to her from Altadena shared something that I feared she would find

8 Unitarian churches, in my experience at that time could lean toward academia, appealing to scientists and scholarly thinkers averse to "spirituality" and talk of God, or they could be more like the Universalists, comfortable with contemplative experiences. The two fellowships merged in 1961.

distasteful. I told her about Harvey Hansen's yoga sessions. I went a step further.

"Louise, have you ever thought about certain concepts that come out of the sacred texts of India?"

Hesitantly I added, "I find myself wondering if I may have lived before. Does this seem odd to you?"

I sealed the letter, stamped it and sent it 2,000 miles to the town that still felt like home, knowing my question could be a friendship cooler.

Within a couple of weeks Louise's return letter showed up in our mailbox among bills and ads. I tore it open. Louise never wrote at length. I always felt her as partially somewhere else, in a sphere behind a veil I couldn't penetrate. I pictured her lovely but sorrowful dark eyes and quiet poise as I read, searching for her answer to my question.

"Not at all," was her response. Suddenly, I saw those eyes light up mischievously as if she were in front of me. I breathed relief. But the words that followed sent a thrill of suspense down my spine.

"I'd like to send something to you."

Louise, the individual I revered, had a talisman for me. What could it be?

Within two weeks a package arrived. Unwrapping it, I took into my hands a weighty book with an orange jacket featuring an androgynous face with penetrating eyes looking into mine. Louise had sent me *The Autobiography of a Yogi*. I was dumbfounded. In the frontispiece she wrote, "With love to Julie. August 12, 1972." Then she added: "p. 490." Upon that page she marked some lines from the Bhagavad Gita, translated poetically by Sir Edwin Arnold:

Steadfast a lamp burns sheltered from the wind;
Such is the likeness of the Yogi's mind
Shut from sense-storms and burning bright to Heaven . . .
Call that state "peace," that happy severance Yoga;
Call that man the perfect Yogin.

Anything Louise said or sent to me bore layers of meaning. When the girls returned to school for their third year in California, Diane entering high school, Katherine and Celeste assigned different campuses each fall to assure black student-white student balance, I opened the *Autobiography* to Chapter One. I felt the excitement of a pilgrim setting foot on the road to Lourdes or Mecca. The author, one of the first yogis from India to settle in California in 1924 after a short time in Boston, was Paramahansa Yogananda.[9] His narrative was clear, down-to-earth and mind-boggling.

I turned pages like one obsessed. He wrote in a matter-of-fact style, telling tales typical of anyone's childhood, but interspersed were accounts of such miraculous happenings that they begged credulity. The author presented stories of the superhuman powers of India's many living sages. His explanations of what he called a "science of the soul" made Jesus, the Christ, appear to shine in a company of endless other mystics performing acts defying Newtonian science. I remembered Jesus's reassuring words to his disciples, *"He that believeth on me, the works that I do shall he do also."*[10] Should I dismiss the tales as fabrication or stretch into a new mindset that could see underlying truths connecting all sacred texts?

---

9 Paramahansa Yogananda came to this country in 1920 from India as a delegate to the International Congress of Religions, sponsored by the liberal Unitarian Church of Boston. He followed Swami Vivekananda, chief disciple of the nineteenth-century mystic Ramakrishna. Vivekananda was the first Hindu yogi to come to America in the fall of 1893, invited to speak to the World's Parliament of Religions in Chicago, introducing Vedanta and yoga to the West.
10 John 14:12. (Bible, King James Version)

With the volume in my hands like an amulet, I overruled my instinctive skepticism of this modern-day saint, Yogananda. He squabbled and teased his many siblings like any kid brother. He also told of friends or family repeatedly mocking his spiritual inclinations. "Don't try so hard to chase after God yet," his older brother would say. "Get a good job first and earn your living."

Reading this amazing book, I felt like a fledgling nudged out of the nest discovering it had wings. Fifty percent or more fall prey to windmills, wires and raptors perched on hidden limbs, of course. But for the moment I soared upward.

21

Three Steps Forward, Two Backward

"Come on, Julie . . . you're going to believe that kind of nonsense, swamis materializing a second body out of nowhere? I give your common sense more credit than that!"

With Peter's liberal family so dismissive of faith-based belief systems, and my own mother a fence-sitting skeptic, I was ill at ease with my new enthusiasms. As I read to him, hoping at least for his curiosity, Peter could hardly listen to the passages from the *Autobiography*.

"Peter, there is a power here, as there is to my new yoga practice. For the first time I feel new footing, new strength at my center." I sounded a little like Nadia.

"Well, it may work for you. It's not for me. If I could believe all that, I could believe *anything*."

He shook his head. For Peter, believing *anything* was tantamount to losing his wits, abandoning the laws of science, the cause-and-effect world of higher learning.

I was on my own. This new phenomenon of yoga and India's ancient wisdom was gently undoing my knots of disbelief the way a magician scissor-snips a tangle of cord, then draws out a perfect unbroken ribbon. Peter might find it all leading into nonsense, but for me it was a way out of craziness.

Diane was going through her own doubly difficult transition. Fiercely loyal to place and playmate, not only had she been forced to shed her Hinsdale world of four distinct seasons and a best friend, but she had rushed through puberty into adolescence. It had torn away her tomboy identity as prince of tetherball. Discovering junior high schoolmates wearing make-up and flirting, she forced herself into a new identity, but a part of her clung to childhood. A budding artist, she took to her room painting abstracts and composing disturbing poems, but rocking horses appeared as a frequent theme, the acrylic color of blood against velvet blackness. Our eldest daughter was in turmoil. My heart ached for her.

As if nature itself were against this uprooting of us Midwesterners, it introduced us rudely to a wind as ferocious as southern France's storied Mistral. No one had warned us about the wind, often referred to in the plural as the "Santa Anas." It could gain speeds up to seventy miles an hour. Our first encounter with the powerful gale was at nighttime. Funneling southward from the desert through the twists of our narrow Eaton Canyon's mountain ravine, it whistled eerily and rustled leaves at first. Suddenly, all the French doors of our home, from which I had removed a bunch of what appeared useless, annoying latches in the molding, began to rattle. Next, every one of them blew open, then slammed shut. The girls woke up whimpering, making a beeline for the hallway nearer our bedroom. All night long the Santa Anas played with our doors like wild instruments, banging and shuddering them up and down. We latched the few latches I hadn't unscrewed, but learned too late my error in throwing the hardware away.

The next day the winds continued. That afternoon, home from school, Diane was in her bedroom looking out her front window at leaves and twig debris whirling past sideward. Suddenly, she gave a cry, calling out to anyone within earshot.

"Come quick! Hurry! The tree, the tree! Hurry!"

By the time I could join her upstairs, our beautiful jacaranda tree had toppled to the ground. There it lay, horizontal, with its spreading green crown crumpled under broken branches. Diane was sobbing. We stood side by side sadly staring at the forty-foot giant humbled by the wind. To see a tree go over, *her* tree shading the front lawn, was symbolic of impermanence. We learned later that we had lived through one of the most powerful Santa Anas in recent years. Nothing endured in this treacherous California!

Within a short period, Altadena suffered a second unnerving event, a significant earthquake. The strong shake following upon the loss of her jacaranda pushed Diane over an edge. In ninth grade at John Muir High School where many of the buildings were heavy stucco structures, she was too afraid to pass through the entry doors. A teacher had joked, "See that crack up there? This 'D' Building could go at any minute." Diane stayed home from classes, shaking, two days in a row. When Peter and I suggested to her the possibility of leaving California for her second high school year, she looked as though we had thrown her a lifesaver. We settled upon the Northfield Mount Hermon School in Northfield, Massachusetts, the town where my father had grown up. The boarding school had a nurturing educational philosophy and a work-study program all students took part in, helping in the kitchen and with the maintenance of the campus. She would start the following year as a sophomore.

Southern California's crumbling slopes and tough-leafed bushes knew tricks of survival we hadn't mastered. We Parkers were all sensitive by nature and would take several years to adapt to our place in a semi-desert. Katherine found the most help during the family's resettlement by embracing activities she could share with her parent.

She was our first daughter to want to join the Camp Fire Girls. I became a Camp Fire "mother," remembering my love of summer camp and Girl Scouts. It cheered me to plan craft activities and hikes up the nearby mountain trail for the seven members. Katherine and I also took ice skating lessons together. She was buddies with her classmates but remained self-contained, slowly building confidence.

I drove Katherine, now eleven, to her weekly ballet classes. She was good company for me at a time when both Diane and Celeste seemed remote, perhaps protecting themselves from maternal intrusion. I still created skating outfits for Katherine and helped her plan music and costumes for the Rotary Club annual talent show. She had a rare intensity about her that could have led to a career on stage or in film. Twice she entered the Rotary's kid's talent contest; twice she won the top prize.

Celeste, almost ten, now was old enough to try various after-school activities as well. She enrolled in piano lessons, but every time she hit a wrong note she winced. The dissonance set her nerves quivering. For Christmas we gave her a wristwatch, but it quit. We exchanged it for another whose hands wouldn't move either. Celeste had a chemistry about her that interfered with the instrument's workings. When she tried karate, however, the lessons were a surprising take for this delicate child. Rolling onto a mat, kicking and punching gave Celeste a measure of new confidence. She weighed so little that she sprang up local mountain trails like a pogo stick, later becoming an avid mountaineer with stamina matching her male friends. The boys in the desegregated school liked her shy smile, and one showed his affection by clipping a lock of her silky long blond hair as she sat unaware at the desk in front of him.

I began to acclimate somewhat to our new area. The barren mountains, so hostile at first, now became interesting at dusk with late rays of sun turning the dips and flanks shades of golden rose-lavender. Sometimes in overcast fog the layers looked like a Chinese scroll painting, with low clouds separating a front range from the brooding steely peak behind it. Then, in a backward moment, I would wake up shaking, rejecting this desiccated soil. I was scared of the hard-caked earth, its bleached pallor, the thorny tongues of weeds mocking my fragility. At such times the memory of my little spring rock garden on York Road with its rose tulips and wild Sweet William created such heartache that I wept. My life force at such times waned, preferring to give up rather than struggle. In the little rocker from army life in Georgia, I would rock and rock. It helped calm the uprooted feeling. I'd read another chapter in the *Autobiography of a Yogi*. Gradually, the sessions of yoga with Harvey were giving me stamina.

A new relationship with Peter emerged, more thoughtful, appreciative and sensual. He loved California's natural wonders. We took trips to Big Bear and Idyllwild, forest communities in the San Gabriel and San Jacinto mountains. Our lovemaking had taken on a new degree of intimacy. The Mariana episode had helped; yoga played its own role, relaxing my taut nerves and muscles.

I noticed, on the back cover of Yogananda's autobiography, mention of an ongoing association founded by the author called Self-Realization Fellowship. There was even a temple I could attend in Hollywood. The timing of my new interest in eastern spirituality couldn't have been more propitious.

The Human Potential movement was mushrooming in a significant segment of society, especially in California. Its timing paralleled stunning reversals in the decades of tension between Russia and the United States. The Berlin Wall was coming down, and Gorbachev was ending the Cold War. Among psychologists, Abraham Maslow felt traditional analysts were putting too much emphasis on pathology in human beings, not enough on an individual's ability to have peak experiences.

Quantum physicists, too, were confronting "consciousness." Their language was incomprehensible to me, but reading books like Fritjof

Kapra's *The Tao of Physics* made me reflect again upon my psychosis. Could the normal mind have a firm, protective consciousness "barrier" that is fragile in the mentally ill? Might there be a connection between the disordered state of the psychotic, overwhelmed by a blast of limitless consciousness, and mystics, who train their minds to enter infinite awareness one step at a time over decades? As enthusiasts for attending annual talks by Krishnamurti in the late 1970s, Peter and I would drive to Ojai, California to join others sitting under a grove of live oaks and hear him address the human condition. He always insisted attendees think for themselves rather than idolize him as guru. His emphasis on logic, approaching the whys of humanity's misery as a philosopher, appealed to Peter, giving us a small bond in my new passion for India.

Men of science, I would read, several of whom lived near us in Pasadena and Altadena as visiting scholars or instructors at the California Institute of Technology were baffled by quantum mechanics, joking they didn't understand it. Theoretical physicist David Bohm liked to converse with Krishnamurti on visits to the sage's Ojai center. Physicist Fritjof Capra embraced the connection between Eastern philosophy and quantum theory, expressing the idea that the mystic, starting from the inner realm and the physicist from the outer world, arrive at the same conclusion.[11]

These observations were reassuring to me because scientists were admitting that the quantum edge of physics was leading into territory that may have overwhelmed me in my sickest moments. In many chapters of the *Autobiography of a Yogi*, the author dove into the nature of mind, describing powers, seemingly miraculous, that can be gained through years of meditation.

Sadly, the Human Potential movement did not enjoy media longevity. Perhaps because quantum theory is too difficult to explain, it had no

11. Capra, Fritjof. *The Tao of Physics*. Boulder, Colorado: Shambhala, 1975, 305

spike like the Covid virus to give the media a grip. The positivism of the era was soon replaced by the digital age, supplying newsmakers with topics of alarm and doom to snare viewer attention.

We began to try some of the more popular weekend destinations our neighbors talked about. With the girls we hiked the Deer Springs trail in Idyllwild. But again, the desolate, gravelly mountain range parched my spirit. Nothing watered the soul here as did Vermont hills or Hinsdale's greenery.

The only bright spot at times, alternating with the fear that I might never learn to adapt to the new environment, was picking up the *Autobiography of a Yogi*. But the exhilaration didn't last. I see-sawed between this strange land of California, feeling transient one moment, then reading a chapter about eternal soul wisdom the next.

One day we drove two hours to the Ramona Bowl Amphitheatre in Hemet at the foot of the San Jacinto Mountains. An extravaganza takes place there every spring, the longest running outdoor stage play in the United States. While watching the pageant, an early California romance, I felt a misery of a kind I could not put my finger on. Part way through the play I wanted to run away, where to, I had no idea, sick to my stomach and scared that old symptoms were gaining rather than receding. The nausea puzzled me.

Upon driving back to Altadena, I realized something was interfering with my menstrual periods. My system felt stressed and unable to overcome a lingering dejection. I made an appointment with a gynecologist, Dr. Gordon Griggs, telling him of the struggles our family was having acclimating to California. He listened with gravity, then examined me. His next words stabbed like an agave leaf.

"I think you're pregnant."

"Well, Cerulea, do things still look propitious?" The Daemon never misses object lessons.

"I admit to feeling the blow a little. More than a little." The Fairy sighs, wings sagging. "You know, it is tiring forever repairing tears in the gossamer."

"Eternity does weigh at times." The Daemon holds a stretch of the veil firmly, working with Cerulea to facilitate the mending. The Fairy looks up, thankful for the Daemon's assistance.

22

No Way Out Again?

It could not be. Shocked at the very word "pregnant," bringing back an earlier Julie, I repeated it, as if in trance. The news threw our lives into renewed consternation.

"Dearest heart. Julie, look at me."

Peter took my face in his palms and gazed into my eyes as if we were parting once again.

"Do you know how precious you are to me, to all of us? Your happiness, your health is all that matters . . ."

He now drew me into his arms, gently stroking my back, a reflex of endearment. His blue eyes, so open and vulnerable, teared slightly. My mind was racing between two options, both possibly lethal. We lay the facts out, examining our choices in the face of this new danger. I was a much more solid person at thirty-seven than I had been at twenty-eight. The depression over our move, still causing me lingering mourning, appeared to be receding. Which would be the greater risk, I worried, giving birth to a fourth child followed by the peril of another hospitalization, or having a therapeutic abortion which might trigger a hormonal or psychological reaction of similar intensity? This new predicament threatened everything that was beginning to fall in place. Peter was heartsick.

"We don't even know if ending this pregnancy is possible," I worried.

In the 1960s, '70s and '80s abortion was illegal in California except in rare cases where the mother's or unborn baby's life appeared endangered. If that were to be the path chosen, we soon learned it would require in my case the opinion and written consent of three psychiatrists. We only knew the psychiatrist I had seen for several visits in the Pasadena area after the Whittier Hospital experience. And would my emotional status be considered life-threatening?

"Maybe I should call Dr. Lacroix and seek his opinion. If we can find his Illinois phone number after all these years." The mention of his name brought back the psychiatrist's cryptic "I don't know."

Peter nodded. "First, let's feel our way through this. We have three beautiful daughters. A baby at this point would be quite a shakeup. On the other hand, you've been talking about liking California more, the yoga thing . . . you could probably handle a newborn if that is your decision."

"Yes, except I'm still having some shaky spells . . ."

"I know. Let's call your parents. Your father could offer medical advice."

My parents' thoughts were firm: I should terminate this pregnancy. My ever-helpful mother and father, approaching their seventies, undoubtedly shrank at the possibility of being saddled with another infant.

Peter and I considered Celeste, emerging from a childhood of aloneness, still shy and in the shadow of her older sisters. I had opened my heart more and more to this fragile child, learning about her special gifts, trying to help her find ways of self-expression.

"Maybe Celeste would enjoy no longer being "my little sister" as Katherine likes to introduce her. Or maybe she would feel thrust aside once again."

A heaviness came over me, with a sense of growing foreboding. The girls, oblivious, were giggling in the den watching *I Love Lucy*, waiting for dinner.

The possibility that this fetus might be the son I had longed for agitated rather than calmed my quandary. Peter never breathed the word "boy" or "gender."

At the heart of our dilemma was an unknown: might a therapeutic abortion cause as much emotional upheaval as giving birth had? Feeling the urgency of time, we knew the many steps it would require to locate and arrange meetings with willing psychiatrists and then schedule a pregnancy termination with Dr. Griggs.

I made a decision. Trying to imagine a renewed depression or worse—a period of non-functionality no matter which option was chosen, I decided it would be easier to work through it without a newborn to care for. Peter agreed. Making our plans now focused upon enlisting Dr. Griggs's guidance to thread our way through California's laws governing abortion. We were headed into another unknown.

"I feel sad and stupid that I let you down, losing my head over that woman. I don't know what came over me."

"You mustn't! It was a wake-up call for me, and the shock I needed. It evened the score somehow to know you could mess up too! I am trying to be a more dependable partner, growing up at last, sharing the work burden . . ."

"You have been the love of my life, my entire happiness. If anything should happen to you, you must know that I will care for our children alone. I could never find anyone I could love as I love you."

"No, Peter. You have to have a companion, and our girls will need a mother figure, especially in their teen years. We have created together what can never be erased by a new partner. There are wonderful human beings everywhere. You are a lover and giving is your nature."

Our San Gabriel foothills were flaunting one of their rare storms, with lightning flashes outlining bushes outside our windows, followed by rumbling thunder rattling our French doors. I went into Celeste's bedroom and then Katherine's, on my nightly rounds to hug the girls good night, but both beds were empty. I found all three huddled together in their oldest sister's bed, and smiled. They had their father and each other for comfort if anything should confiscate their mother again.

As we renewed our vows under the bed covers, the rest of the world, even our own daughters, had no interest in what was transpiring. A giant shakeup in values was altering America all around us. Our neat and orderly society was crumbling, along with laws that were causing the very crisis enmeshing Peter and me. Rules and taboos we had grown up with were dissolving like sand castles before waves of protest and marches of outrage over Vietnam. But the idea of abortion as anathema, murder, shame, still persisted. The traditions that had formed us bumped up against the cusp of the sixties' revolution.

Dr. Griggs, a physician of good sense and long experience, had his own suggestion when I told him of my mental illness history.

"Well, then, I think the best thing is for us to perform a hysterectomy. You have a nice family, and removing your uterus will avoid all possible repetition of pregnancies."

This was bitter news, spiking anxiety over how my hormones might respond to a much dicier surgical procedure than abortion. Dr. Griggs reassured me that I could be given a mega-dose of estrogen to avoid early menopause. With ovaries still in place, he wagered the chances were low of a relapse into emotional illness symptoms.

Resigned, and with the surgeon's help, I made appointments with two psychiatrists, both of whom listened to my story and wrote diagnoses of the type that would convince any state board this pregnancy would endanger me, my present children and a new infant. One scribbled "schizophrenia." Dr. Lacroix, whom we contacted by phone as the needed third physician, was the greatest problem.

"I'm Catholic, Mrs. Parker. This is difficult for me. I'm opposed to abortion in principle."

I was adamant. "But Dr. Lacroix, I have struggled and finally healed, and we are now a functioning family with three wonderful daughters. Wouldn't it be folly to risk endangering all of this with another possible postpartum psychosis? No one knows better than you what I went through at Forest Hospital."

Dr. Lacroix reflected silently, then reluctantly agreed.

Mother came out to help Peter with the girls during the week I was in the hospital. Dr. Griggs gave me a huge shot of an estrogen-pro-gesterone concoction, and reported proudly that he had repaired torn muscles from births that had left my skinny pelvic area with a deep vertical furrow. He removed my appendix and a cyst on one ovary that was pre-cancerous. All the defense I had left between me and early menopause was the remaining ovary.

The hysterectomy had more benefits than drawbacks. There was now little risk of ovarian cancer, no chance of appendicitis. Sexual intimacy now freed itself from its biological purpose. I started hormone replacement therapy, and, coupled with the soothing effects of yoga, my recovery never sank into the nightmare terrain I had dreaded.

23

Self-Realization Takes Root

"You're beginning to relax, and yoga is helping you become more limber. Here, let me work on your back a little. Just lie still and relax."

Yoga sessions with Harvey Hansen's students alone in his tiny house bred in him familiarity. He looked forward to my visits. For me the postures were creating a romance with India's sacred wisdom. For Harvey, the romance was of another nature. The red feather was rising.

Whether it was my own potential for eros, reminding me of the Walt episode in France, or Harvey's betraying his trust as my teacher, I tightened immediately.

"No, Harvey. No. I don't want a massage."

Things were entering a troubling stage. Without "explaining or complaining," I never returned.

Still, due to Harvey's approach to Hatha philosophy, emphasizing meditative surrender, I was overcoming an inherent guardedness. As my rigidity melted, something wonderful had been happening. At age thirty-eight, the tight bud of my sexuality bloomed. For Peter and me there was now a thrilling connecting, he as thruster entrusting himself to the receiver, I, as receiver, entrusting myself to the thruster. A period of wild conjugal passion blossomed. Our energies and magnetism for one another rivaled the intensity of illicit lovers.

A more Freudian interpretation startled me. Had I, at age three perhaps, when baby Jay entered our family, developed a pernicious case of penis envy, buried at my core? Surrounded with brothers, did I worry my mother loved them best? Is it possible I wanted what they had so badly, totally dismissive of my own inverted genitals, that I unconsciously cut off all males' lower half in my envy or fury? And what about that intense disappointment at the birth of each daughter? Had I hoped to acquire the coveted appendage indirectly through the birth of a son?

Is this part of many women's unconscious longing?

When my insight finally unmasked this self-defeating envy warp, I laughed for an hour. There was only one way to possess that penis, and that was to share my partner's. It shocked me to realize that this twist may have played a role in a psychosis that nearly destroyed me after the birth of a third daughter. I was desperate for union, for joy, for the end of loneliness, for a capacity to give and receive intimately. Instead, sex for me had been laden with a tot's repressed jealousy and frigid misery.

Diane asked one day, "Mama, aren't you going to go visit that 'Fellowship' you talked about?"

"Will you go with me if I try a Sunday?"

"Sure. Let's go this weekend."

"Julie. Is that a wise move?" Peter was not enthusiastic. In his view this yogi had created a fringe religion. "You're getting into this yoga thing deeper." He said no more.

The following Sunday morning Diane and I headed for Hollywood, the original Self-Realization Fellowship (SRF) Temple on Sunset Boulevard. The service was very strange for a Protestant or Unitarian. Each attendee sat stiffly in meditation with closed eyes, palms on thighs, now and then chanting to the tune of a hand-held lap organ. The ochre-robed brother leading us was playing it, hitting wrong notes, eyes closed in meditation as well. A long silence followed before he delivered a brief lesson from "Master's teachings." When the monk dismissed us, after a final "Om Shanti Amen" in unison, each person rose, walked out of the sanctuary silently, and looked neither right nor left. No socializing was encouraged; no collection plate had been passed.

On the ride home we shared views.

"Didn't it seem odd to you, on that panel behind the leader, to see the painting of Jesus up there among all those gurus with Indian names," I asked.

"Well, you've been telling us in the book you're reading that Yogananda keeps talking about miracles in the Bible, and he explains them as though they happen in India pretty regularly. What's the big deal?"

Diane was disappointed the experience hadn't been more exotic.

Her response to this bizarre hour of sitting in a pew next to others turned inward encouraged me. Our children had not had a traditional church exposure. They were ignorant of Protestant ways of worship. As we drove home, I wondered whether to try attending a second time..

"Well? How was it?" Peter tried to sound neutral.

"It was strange, very strange. But Diane didn't seem to think so. She might be willing to go again."

"If I were you, I would be very careful before getting more involved. Remember, Harvey Hansen couldn't keep to his noble yoga principles!"

"That's true. But I had the good sense to leave him. Yoga comes out of one of the great world philosophies."

"You are right, but it's not for me. Not at all. Never." Peter turned to walk out of the hallway as if he might become infected.

I caught his hand. "It doesn't have to be for you. I love you for what you believe. If you suddenly flipped and became a 'born again' I'd really panic."

Peter smiled. "Do we have anything planned for lunch or shall we go out to El Torito?" He liked the short drive to that colorful Mexican restaurant.

My partner, however, faced a dilemma. His wife was dabbling in a field his scientific bent could not respect. Now it threatened to influence his daughters. He decided to seek out the Unitarian Church in Pasadena, interrupting his happy ritual of mowing the lawn on Sundays. He went alone a few times to make a point.

The timing of my discovery of Eastern philosophy coincided with a wave of young adult frenzy all around us. Directed against the Vietnam War draft, the fury challenged our government's actions with wild student outbursts on college campuses. We were stunned to read that rioters at the University of California, Santa Barbara had set fire to the local Bank of America. Where was the chancellor? Colleges seemed paralyzed, yielding to student ultimatums.

"If you can send us to die in Vietnam, you can't tell us to be in bed by 10 p.m.!" was the common cry, erasing forever the Silent Generation's unquestioning obedience to elders.

Parietal hours and university responsibility for student behavior crumpled overnight. New counterculture "groupies" were gathering in pot-smoking communes, traveling around in cast-off buses, some forming the famous Hog Farm that helped put on the Woodstock Music Festival of 1969. Quiet suburban Hinsdale now seemed part of a Pollyanna existence.

Our daughters and I were like the loose stones that Chicagoans joked rolled to the West Coast. Katherine and Celeste, twelve and eleven, became fascinated along with Diane with the sudden hippie movement springing up everywhere. I loved its focus on the spiritual wisdom of India.

One weekend in Laguna Beach we headed like magnets to *Icarus Is,* a tiny shack perched on the edge of the Pacific, a store smelling of Patchouli Oil, advertising mystical arts and India print bedspreads. Sitar sounds on a strangely sliding music scale floated out from the dark interior. The girls bought beads and leather pouches with cheap crystals to hang around their necks while I bought Alan Watts' *The Way of Zen* and *The Hero with a Thousand Faces* by Joseph Campbell. Peter was waiting for us outside by a store with geologic rock samples in its windows. As soon as we got home, we put on an LP record I had selected by Tony Scott playing his jazz clarinet in *Music for Zen Meditation.* I love it to this day, a little scratched.

Life had a carnival aspect in the late 1960s and '70s. Hare Krishna devotees with shaved Mohawks and orange gowns danced and chanted with tambourines on street corners, handing out leaflets. Gurus pouring over from Asia found new converts on U.S. soil. Among these monastics came Swami Satchidananda with Integral Yoga; Sri Chinmoy with his message of peace at the heart of individuals; Amrit Desai, founder of the Kripalu Center, and Sri Rajneesh, who went off the deep end in Oregon. Swami Muktananda gave seekers "Shaktipat" enlightenment with a tap of a peacock feather. Newspapers loved it, mocking the saffron robes and reporting every whisper of impropriety as front-page news. Self-Realization Fellowship had preceded this whole wave by forty years; Paramahansa Yogananda's following avoided major scandal.

We now had a leg in two worlds, mourning the seasons and friends of Hinsdale while feeling excitement in the dynamism of Southern California. Still, I had setbacks when memories of the hospital would revisit me. At such times I would shudder and question again whether I could ever heal.

Within a few months I had become quite anchored in Self Realization Fellowship. Diane, Katherine and Celeste absorbed some
mooring through their mother's newfound spirituality, but it thrust
them into the counterculture, inspired by orange-robed personalities
from India. This gave our three daughters a slight precociousness. I did
not want these sisters to suffer from my terror of sexuality, a part of
me only recently coming into its own. My liberalism, however, left our
girls unprotected from the "make love not war" opportunism running
rampant. Later they reported devastating early experiences, blaming
me for lack of supervision.

Meditation was all the rage. I was meditating for longer and longer
periods. Wanting my own sacred spot, I looked the house over for a
suitable corner and identified a pass-through rectangle off our bedroom.
This bit of hallway led to both our bathroom and the upstairs open
space above our garage, prosaic, unassuming. It needed a symbol.

Diane was in love with art. She painted continuously while enrolling
in ceramics classes during her one and only year at Muir High School
before heading to Northfield Mount Hermon across the country. I
asked her if she might paint on this door to the outside balcony a
Self-Realization Fellowship cross, a Christian cross superimposed with
a golden lotus blossom and star representing a single eye.[12]

"Sure," she responded.

That very weekend Diane brought her tools—paint brushes, rulers,
acrylic colors in light blue, yellow, and gold—up to the little alcove
with a floor lamp for light. It took her from morning until dusk. I did
not come near this teenaged alchemist to inspect or interfere. When
she finished, she called to me. I mounted the stairs and entered our
bedroom, circling the bed toward the alcove. I took a step back. There,
to my astonishment, was a symbol almost blinding me. The blue cross

---

12 There is a reference to this eye in the Bible: "If, therefore, thine eye be single, thy whole body
   shall be full of light." King James Version: Matthew 6:22

radiated while its yellow lotus and centered golden star quivered as though alive. The little square of space, that humble pass-through to the upstairs porch, had been transfigured. Diane had created a living emblem. She took her paints and left the cubicle, mission accomplished. I remembered the saying, "*The one who carves the Buddha never worships it.*" We all went downstairs to a special dinner I had prepared. No wonder I feel a numinous bond with my eldest daughter.

When Peter's sister Gwen and her husband Nirmal, a professor at Sonoma State University, came to visit I showed them the alcove. Gwen had married a Sikh who had shed all things India with a scoff, including the turban.

"Oh, Aunt Jool," he teased, drawing out my nickname, "all that running after saffron robes is old school in India. India kicks them out and they head for America."

Nirmal was quite earthy. My love of the spiritual wisdom integral to his native land amused him.

"You know, all those gurus come out of meditation when they have to poop, just like you and me."

For a while I continued to attend Self Realization Fellowship services, but gradually I connected to SRF only through meditation, practicing a technique of observing my inhaling and exhaling, sometimes for an hour or more.

One day, deeply pulling air out of the cosmos and releasing it back to where it came from, I felt my atoms separate from their neighbors. Before I could anchor myself, a vision appeared. My awareness had penetrated through common wavelengths into the between, maybe, of quantum physics. It made contact with an ethereal, unstable vibration as authentic as a faint radio wave. Momentarily time split open and allowed Yogananda's guru and his companion to appear before me from some rarified ether. Thrilled, I rushed forward mentally and the two vanished.

Newton's laws, however, keep their promise. I went downstairs to find eggs exploded all over the kitchen walls and ceiling. It was a kind of warning. "Pull back, you have a family that likes egg salad sandwiches."

The Cerulean Fairy's wings vibrate at the speed of light. "Daemon, my faithful ally, you surely now see our protagonist approaching the Final Goal!"

"Our protagonist is indeed overflowing with self. It is flooding her forward."

"It is so inspiring to watch! You must agree, Daemon."

"Such an inundation concerns more than inspires. It often signals reversal."

"Well, you are the friend of relapses. Let them come!"

"Let's not invite them. The closer one comes to the Final Goal, the more risk there is of 'almosts.' Steady, Cerulea. Each step forward adds a straw that can cause breakdown or breakthrough.

24

Teacher, Then Student

"Diane, are you sure you still want to go?" I asked our daughter, half teasing.

"Come on, Mama . . . you know I can't change my mind now."

Our eldest was about to leave home for Northfield Mount Hermon 4,000 miles across the continent. Preparing for her departure saddened me. It was the end of her girlhood, her recognition that childhood had closed forever. She didn't communicate her feelings or worries directly; they passed through her paintbrush onto canvas or poetry onto paper, creating her own solace.

My fifteen-year-old daughter and her father boarded the plane in Los Angeles, landed in Manchester, New Hampshire and said their goodbyes in Northfield, Massachusetts. Peter returned with pictures of their separation. We all sat down to watch. One was a photo of our smiling firstborn, full of hope, looking at her father and waving. The last slide was of a tiny, distant figure from the back, our Diane, walking bravely alone, away from her father as she moved toward a cold stone building with rows of institutional windows. It was too much for me. I couldn't stop crying. Finally, I smiled. She was headed to a place without earthquakes where she could develop artist skills: ceramics, painting, poetry. Her sisters envied her.

Katherine and Celeste were pairing up in public middle school with classmates of all colors, needing us parents mainly for homework help. My California depression had given way to a new energy. Driving homeward up Allen Avenue at dusk, I felt a warmth seep into me as the fading sunset cast rose and golden tints upon the rocky foothill outcroppings behind our home. These were mine! At last I belonged. My ears could no longer hear the strange echo of cars climbing upward, reverberating off the crumbling granite mountain walls.

Four years earlier, in that relapse in Whittier triggered by the rejection of *I, Llewester*, another layer had cracked and peeled off me like a reptilian skin. What had emerged was a startling "strength-of-God" Julie, coursing eventually with life and vitality. I loved this new me, seeking creative ways to reach out, share, expand. The first of several mini careers called to me almost immediately upon Peter's return from delivering Diane. A tiny notice in the *Pasadena Star News* caught my attention.

"Instructors: Private school seeks part-time French and English teacher."

I inquired about the hours, which dovetailed with Katherine and Celeste's return from public school at 4 p.m. Peter was enthused to see me put my skill to use, hoping yoga would pass as an infatuation. I talked with the director about his expectations and was hired.

Oakhurst School, in a rented homey one-story former apartment complex circling a brick patio, was far from an elite choice for parents. Yet it had areas of academic excellence. I was a stickler for grammar, vocabulary, spelling, and reading comprehension with steady drilling. The school attracted teens with attention deficits or learning challenges public school classes couldn't address. Among my ninth graders, Eloise picked upon Zinnie, whose shoulders bent inward over a short frame.

Zinnie had a vivid imagination she poured into science fiction stories, but she couldn't write legibly or string words into a sentence. She straightened up and smiled when I urged her to keep creating her tales, explaining she would need a good secretary.

It wasn't long before students, especially clownish Kory, discovered my interest in yoga.

"Mrs. Parker, did you watch *Kung Fu* last night?" Kory's eyes lit up. "Did you see the part with Master Po?"

The popular TV series followed Caine, a wandering martial artist whose blind Shaolin Master appears to him in flashbacks.

"No, tell me, what was it about this time?" The sage's quotes were always variations of lines from the *Tao Te Ching* or *Zen Flesh Zen Bones*, books on my home shelves.

"Caine is all upset because he sees stupid war all around him."

"And what does Master Po tell him?"

"He says . . . here, I wrote it down . . . he says *Under heaven, all can see beauty as beauty only because there is ugliness. All can know good as good only because there is evil* . . . Do you believe that Mrs. Parker?"

I tried a little of the Tao's indirect teaching, delighted with the teens seeing me as wise adult. "Seek not to know the answers, but to understand the questions."

I had thrown myself into teaching without much forethought, determined to make school fun and a connection to my love of writing and France. Slowly, though, my energy waned. By November of the third year at Oakhurst, vague symptoms, visions again, began to float through my brain with a chilling reminder of that escape from Army life home to Detroit with my first infant in my arms. I reacted quickly, alerting the headmaster that I must break our contract.

The students were devastated. "Why, Mrs. Parker? Don't you like us?"

The next day I came to class with a rock and a paper butterfly I had cut out, colored yellow and rose-edged blue.

"Do you see this butterfly? Well, that is me, your Mrs. Parker. I have lots of ideas, but I am rather fragile."

I set the cutout gently on my desk. Then I clapped the rock down on the little piece of paper.

"Sometimes life feels like this rock, and it gets too hard for me. I love you guys, and I love teaching. But I exhaust myself. I'm learning how to protect my energy."

They were sad. I was sad, but pleased to make a decision that showed I was learning to obey warning signs. Within a month of turning in books, lesson plans, keys, and meeting the new French teacher, my symptoms subsided. The students have managed to keep in touch with their unusual teacher to this day.

The Pasadena City College catalog of classes arrived in the mail offering a morning class on campus called *Man's Religions*. I enrolled and soon was enthralled with our instructor. He was a diminutive man whose eyes sparkled at each new unit: Shintoism, Hinduism, Buddhism, Islam, Judeo-Christianity. He strode back and forth, arms waving, eyes scrutinizing his inner encyclopedia for something to scribble on the board. Then he would whirl around as if touched by his selected quotes. All the faiths seemed sacred to him.

During the chapter on Hinduism, Dr. S. mentioned the phenomenon of swamis pouring into California from India. When I shared that I was practicing yoga, still rare in the early 1970s, he suggested I give a demonstration. There was little room in the modest classroom, but students, eager for distraction, offered to shove furniture toward the back wall. Rather than feeling the weirdness of the setting, I felt pleased to share a routine that had helped me.

Following my instructions, the next week a girl and boy about nineteen and two class members my age arrived in jogging outfits with beach towels. A scraping of desks created a clearing. Shoeless, we spread out our five towels. Totally relaxed and as if I had taught yoga all my life, I began explaining the movements as Harvey Hansen had, starting with standing postures. My voice had a quieting quality to it that I hardly recognized. The atmosphere was hushed; we five did some simple bends, then got down on our hands and knees and ended the demo with the five of us lying flat on the floor on our backs in a final Savasana, or "death posture." Words volunteered themselves. I talked about lying on the earth as it holds us, and how we give it no mind, yet trust it will always be there for us. One thought led to another. I mentioned our breathing, and how we take it for granted as well, letting it go on the exhale, knowing it will be there for our next inhale. I encouraged the four to relax and sink into the earth we usually ignore while it humbly holds up our loftiest buildings. My images grounded me; perhaps others as well.

I segued the group back to our classroom. The five of us had momentarily been in another world. As the class ended, the two nineteen-year-olds stopped me by the door.

"Do you teach this somewhere?"

I thought for a moment. "No, I don't. But I suppose I could."

Dr. S. said, "You have something here, Mrs. Parker. You may want to offer classes."

I shared with Peter, who had shown only modest interest in my written papers, the students' enthusiasm over the demo and the teacher's suggestion.

"Good, sweetheart," he mumbled, opening the mail.

25

Yoga, Peter and the Living Room

"In our living room? Who will these people be? Just anybody who happens to read your ad?" Peter's voice and tightened brow reflected his distaste for strangers. The evening peace he so loved with family was suddenly threatened.

"But look at this giant space we hardly use. It is perfect for group yoga." I was glancing about in the middle of the lofty enclosure, imagining eager bodies lying on mats. I would need to supply towels. And serve tea in a circle. Oh, and copy Harvey's stick figures on a flyer to help students remember. And have calming music barely audible. Easy. Tony Scott's Zen meditation album. Oh, and have everyone wear clothes that stretched. And fill out a disclaimer form. The picturing frothed to the boiling point. Exuberance! I loved the feeling. Leading yoga sessions would center me. I'd share what I loved from my own inner space.

His wife's absorption with Eastern philosophy was creeping like an oil spill over what was precious to Peter: our time together. Yoga was a new rival, and one that didn't play fair.

"I don't know, Julie. I know yoga has helped you a lot, but it seems to be taking over our lives more and more. I want to be supportive, but . . ."

"You are more than supportive, Peter. You have been wonderful with my every undertaking! This plan does nip into our home life a little, but just once or twice a week. From five to six. I'll screen people over the phone. And I'll have dinner prepared before the session."

Smiling with my eager, pleading look, I noticed my partner balking more than usual.

"It's so foreign to everything I was brought up to believe. Why do we need to have people come here? Isn't there a YMCA nearby? How about the Victory Park Community Center or a church?" For a moment we both remembered my French classes in the Unitarian Sunday School building.

"But look, Peter. It's free space we hardly use. In those places I'd have to share a room and pay rent."

"I'm aware of that sweetheart, but, oh, I don't know . . . having classes in our own living room? I have to say that the idea just doesn't appeal to me."

"Peter, I have embraced your family's intellectualism, casting aside my Protestant upbringing without a quiver. I love your clear thinking. And your world view and logic. But I've discovered a path that means a lot to me. It goes beyond the limits of science. People in that class really responded to my demo."

My husband was perturbed. It was harder than usual to finesse this invasion of our family privacy. But he practiced what he believed in, democracy in his relationships.

The biggest rebuff I or the girls ever got was a lecture.

"Well, if you want to do this, go ahead . . . give it a try. Let's see how it goes. You'll probably be good at it. Just don't let people hang around and talk all night."

Peter retreated into the comfort of the den and sat down in his swivel chair at his desk with *Time Magazine*. Katherine came in for help with an algebra equation. With his reluctant okay and my eyes open to a new venture that felt almost consecrated, I stood under the archway gazing into our massive living room. Its heavily braced oak beam ceiling lent a sense of solemnity I had never noticed before.

Our few belongings, spindly New England antiques, huddled themselves around a giant brass coffee table from India that had been left by the former owners. This little suite, two captains' chairs, the pine sofa bed and a couch we had bought, looked like dollhouse furniture beside the circular table and fireplace with its jutting curved mantel stretching to the ceiling. More than half of the rectangular enclosure, the part nearest me standing on the threshold, was empty except for a beige wool rug covering the wood floor. French doors and a giant picture window looked out upon our Chinese elm tree weeping gracefully against a backdrop of the San Gabriel Mountains.

I now saw this imposing structure for what it was. With its hefty crisscrossing girders supporting a two-story cathedral ceiling, the space was meant for activities beyond the ordinary. Was this living room not reminiscent of those medieval chateaus that had private family chapels? A sudden excitement seized me. Like Cervantes mocking his crazy knight Quixote, I began dancing about merrily at my new undertaking while proceeding in dead earnest.

Peter came out into the brick hall and stepped up onto the living room's wooden threshold. He put his arm around me, almost as if holding on to a fleeting life. Were we drifting apart?

"I love you, my darling one. I just don't know what to make of this new direction. It's such an antithesis to everything I believe."

"I value your skepticism, Peter, and your scientific mind so much . . . you're the love of my life. Still, I'd like you to see there has to be *some* value to Eastern philosophy, and not dismiss it entirely. You know I am intelligent, and even basically skeptical myself."

"I know. I want you to try your classes."

"Yoga and meditation have done so much for my confidence, Peter. I hope they have helped me be more thoughtful, more giving."

I should have stopped there. I continued, "Something very powerful happens deep inside me. It's an experience on a cosmic level."

Talk like this made Peter cringe.

"As I said, go ahead."

With those five words of Peter's second okay, rimmed with resignation, the two of us, for the next decades, would enter into an uneasy triangle with a room that had its own transformative power. The living room was nearly free-standing, communicating with the rest of our home—basically a cube with a dining room, study and kitchen below, four bedrooms above—only by the archway into it from the front hall. Peter's den faced it on the other side of the sunken brick entryway with its handsome iron banister rising up the stairs. In this lofty spaciousness, I christened my new venture *Move Gently, Move Mountains*.

The next two decades would float me, week after week, yoga session by yoga session, on a sea of serenity between floor and ceiling. For Peter it was a long, mildly irritating period that drove a small splinter between us. The "Innercise" era, a word I came up with to differentiate my approach to yoga postures from its military opposite, "exercise," tested his endurance for what made me happy. He sacrificed small homey pleasures, waiting patiently at seven behind his sliding door to hear the front portal close upon the last hangers-on. He even participated in an occasional session. But the stretching moves fought with the sinews and tendons of his body, seeming to warn, "Careful. Don't abandon logic." My deep emphasis on "let the earth hold you" suggested a comforting mother to me. Peter had *had* a soothing mother. And earth for him was a medium that he would hoe, dig and plow to earn validation from a stern father. On another level it awed him with its grandeur, like the volcanic Mt. Rainier he had summited twice, a *mother* of a climb.

The major player in this triangle, however, was our living room itself. If it had a tongue, it would tell its own tale. It was a sanctuary without rival. Misused and minimized by failed dreams and squabbles of a string of divorced families owning our home before us, it was a monument to human potential, calling to the higher selves in all of us. A stillness hovered in it like the cloistered quiet of an ancient priory. When I come across students who remember attending sessions in the 1980s, a question brightens them: "Do you still live in the house with that wonderful living room? I used to come home after yoga feeling the world was okay. It was like a temple."

Hundreds joined (well, maybe 300 over four decades) and stayed for a while, then continued on to more rigorous exercise systems. Innercise, or meditation in motion, was hard for Americans. Moving gently to move mountains was slow and disciplined. The alternation between consciously tightening a limb or joint by watching one's mind send a "directive," holding tension a moment, and then letting the energy all empty out was challenging. The leg, arm, or torso would sink back in total relaxation onto the rug. Then, a new effort would be required from the mind, again sending a message along the physical motor nerves as one lay supine. "Leg, I tell you to lift off the floor." The leg responded by rising and holding tension, growing more uncomfortable in the air. "Leg, I tell you to lower and rest on the floor." The relaxed leg felt relief from the effort, giving a sensation of pleasure to the mind in a feedback loop. With such focus, one's mind became absorbed in the beauty of the present, where life is truly lived.

For newcomers seeking novelty and variety, Innercise disappointed. As a guide I offered a set routine of different postures, always in the same order, based on Harvey Hansen's method but connected into a kind of dance. Week in and week out, flowing from one asana[13] to another like Tai Chi, the ritual became as second nature as hands on a steering wheel. My goal was to ingrain this set of moves in every

13. Asana is the Sanskrit word for "pose" or "posture."

person so they could take the experience with them wherever they moved, even share it any way they wished. Students made the routine their own rather than looking to me for "correctness."

The idea that there is one right way, emphasized in many yoga approaches, encouraged dependence upon the teacher as authority in my opinion. I felt this outward focus blocks the inward connection needed to observe what is happening in one's mind as it interacts with one's body. Repeating this observation often enough facilitates a transition from ordinary awareness to a state of slightly altered perception: meditation. The word yoga derives from the Sanskrit word "yug" or "jug," meaning "yoke." The idea is that yoga, if practiced long enough, serves as a yoke. But to what, to whom? It yokes the lost and lonely individual, longing for union, to infinite consciousness, the Tao, Atman, God or whatever word one chooses for ultimate reality.

I often moved with closed eyes, encouraging the group to feel what was happening inside themselves. What the regular attendees loved most was our time lying on the rug in Savasana, totally relaxed, as words of spontaneity emerged from my lips. Recorded for friends who wanted one of these meditations when they felt stressed, these short transpersonal reveries would describe us on our small planet floating in space, reminding us that our worries are truly insignificant on the scale of the universe.

As I look back on those years, I see an experience a little Arthurian, as if we, the faithful seven or so that stayed with me over four decades, were not "knights of the round table," but "maintainers of the Mandala." We moved in a powerful pattern under the gothic vault of that extraordinary space. Our dusky rose towels were arranged evenly like petals around the center point, a circular ornamental tray with its blue floral band surrounding a moonlike mirror at its heart. Sitting upon that mirror flickered three candles in their translucent Capiz shells. Our eyes would meet occasionally, but we were each in our own worlds, making a small contact with our eternal selves.

"*Our protagonist is expanding, flowering beautifully!*" The Cerulean Fairy looks forward to a break in infinite reweaving.

"*Yes. But watch carefully, Cerulea. The Way is now quickening.*"

"*I know what you are thinking . . . it is at these points that things can lose equilibrium.*"

"*There are always signs. We must gird ourselves.*"

The Cerulean Fairy observes the Daemon reining in enthusiasm, remembering the endless protagonists who fail within reach of the Final Goal.

26

The Yoke, 1978

"I guess I'll just go my own way, climbing mountains. I wait and wait, but you're always saying, 'just a minute.' You don't really want to share what I do. We're like trains passing in the night." The cliché fit.

Peter's shoulders sagged. He was a successful businessman enjoying money management, but finances and office work did not feed his spirit. He hated the freeway commute. Night after night he came home and worked at his desk going through the mail, organizing bills for tax records, watching news, waiting for the break in my daily routine that would bring my focus to our partnership. It didn't come.

"Want me to read a chapter to you in *Cosmos?* You love Carl Sagan." He enjoyed practicing reading out loud. Dyslexia persisted, but it was like the limp or stutter one hardly notices in a family member.

"In a minute," I would hear myself responding. I was preparing a weekend retreat in the local mountains for yoga students.

The company that Peter headed had completed the massive project of lifting the midsection of the Fremont Bridge in Portland, Oregon. He had been there, with employees, at one of the four corners, watching the slow elevation, inch by inch, of the 6,000-ton stretch of steel across the Willamette River. The center span had required nerve-racking coordination of thirty-two hydraulic jacks, eight at each corner, lifting it to the connecting spans waiting on either side of the riverbank. Daily newspapers had given it front-page attention for weeks as crowds watched. After that excitement, the return to routine was lackluster. The two of us were entering a valley exposing our deepening distance from each other.

"I know I can plan hiking with a friend or volunteer Saturdays at the Mt. Wilson Observatory, but I don't want our love and closeness to fade."

Tears filled my eyes. I ran to him and threw my arms around him. "Peter, you're the true yogi. When I see you sitting in the den reading, enjoying a peaceful evening, I want to be in there beside you!"

"Maybe. But your time is filled with your own friends and projects. And my contribution at work has passed its peak. There's not much future for me there anymore."

Then Peter's voice grew heavy. He looked at me intently. "I've been thinking and thinking. I want you to know my thoughts."

"Your thoughts?"

"I am planning to resign from the company."

"Resign?" This news showed I was out of touch with the man I loved. "To do what?"

"I really want to go back to school. For a master's degree. You don't show much interest in money. We have enough to live on for a couple of years and you keep claiming disinterest in 'things of this earth.' I think we can swing it."

I had been joking that all I needed was a loin cloth.

"What a super idea, Peter! A master's degree! But where will you enroll?"

Change excited me, especially one initiated by my predictable partner.

"I've been looking into the Drucker School of Management at Claremont University. It's a graduate program designed specifically for people with business experience. Peter Drucker himself will be one of our instructors. I know now where my management weaknesses are. Maybe afterward I'll look for a small company of my own. Maybe by then you'll be done with India, and we can plan weekends together.

I was as pleased as Peter about the plan. At forty-seven, Peter had much to offer. The Drucker classes were scheduled at night for working people. Peter could study during the day and leave about 3 p.m. for the campus.

That fall my husband began a year of study, gaining practical skills and enjoying rapport among fellow managers with various degrees of expertise. At the time, Peter Drucker's principles of how to run a successful organization were counter-intuitive for old-style bosses hanging onto power. Conversations with the legendary guru vibrated with his comments around the long table in the plush room where students enjoyed a formal dinner. Peter returned home quoting the master.

"Drucker has so much common sense. He talked tonight about how successful leaders are not afraid of strength in others. He made his point with a quote from Andrew Carnegie."

I loved this man, suddenly so alive. "Carnegie? Why Carnegie?"

"I guess Carnegie wanted to put on his gravestone something about not fearing to hire men with more ability than he had himself. I can't believe I have this chance to study with Drucker. He's in his eighties, you know."

The program ended all too soon, thrusting Peter into the next stage, the world of work beyond a campus. His search stretched out for months, finally locating a small hydraulic and pneumatics business where he could apply the skills he had acquired at Claremont.

For the next ten years, my husband and a co-owner, a salesman he had engaged from an earlier association, ran this business with a crew of fourteen. Gradually, saving and investing a large portion of his salary, Peter was preparing for the biggest change of his adult life. When his partner, who was seven years older, wanted to retire, Peter came home preoccupied one night.

"You know, I'm really tired of life in Los Angeles. I've never liked cities."

"Well, let's talk about the situation," I said cheerfully without a thought of caution. "I want us both to be happy with our chosen paths. How can we do things differently?"

What Peter said next reflected his real dilemma. Disheartened words came out one by one of how our union was failing him. I was still wrapped up in yoga, having just finished a thirteen-part instructional television program called *Move Gently, Move Mountains*, and was now talking about a commercial video.

"I feel I'm pulling our married life alone. It's like there's no partner beside me. I'm in the yoke built for two, but the other side is empty."

That night in bed we sat against our pillows plumped together talking about our sadness, our differences, his unmet needs, my immersion in a belief system that repelled him. We mourned together our lost closeness. We admitted our separateness. Peter pointed out the incongruity of me claiming to be deeply in love, yet choosing yoga involvement over companionship with him. This frankness brought out resoluteness. Peter began to visualize what *he* wanted.

"Here we are in this beautiful state of California and we hardly ever visit the desert or Yosemite or the redwood country. And we both love Vermont, for God's sake. We would never have met if it hadn't been for Middlebury."

These words were rousing. Ferocity surfaced in response to the injustice I suddenly saw in my own self-centeredness and my partner's patience, waiting for that day when we would pull together. The mention of Vermont was salve to the soul.

For years we had been returning to New England summer after summer. We would spend half a month at my parents' colonial vacation home and woods in Clarendon, the Vermont farm they had purchased the year we moved to California. Then we would drive across the state line for the rest of our free time to Peter's family's lakeside camp in New Hampshire. But in both settings, relatives—humanity—split us from the solace of our own privacy and a relationship with wilderness. Peter was homesick for a connection to land, to trees, to hands-on work that had built his self-esteem, the boy who couldn't read.

My native impatience became the agent of change. Without knowing it, I was about to create the perfect set-up for confronting my deepest character flaws. We were on our way to my parents' summer farm in Clarendon, Vermont.

Alone in one twin bed, whispering furiously to Peter in the other of the two creaking antiques in the blue flowered bedroom my mother always assigned to us on vacation, I practically spat out the words.

"I'll be damned if we'll come back one more time to a summer spot that isn't ours. We are going to look for our own place in Vermont!"

The idea had sizzled to the surface after a particularly frustrating walk in the Clarendon woods with my father. Peter had had his chainsaw in hand; he had seen pines that needed thinning, young maples that could be pruned, stagnant puddles in ditches with no drainage. As he itched to tackle a project, my father equivocated on where to start. Peter walked back to the farm silent and downcast, shovel and saw dangling in his powerful hands.

I raged inside. We would look for a piece of Vermont woods where Peter and I together could steward our own square of wilderness! We would honor *his* passion, but one we shared. We would look for a little farm. We'd work together in our own woods. I'd plant a garden.

That very summer, Peter and I began checking out modest places with some forest acreage and a camp or cabin we could fix up. We were crossing a threshold. All three daughters were young adults, Diane and Celeste sharing an apartment pursuing graduate degrees and Katherine married. Within the next few years Peter would decide to sell his business. I hummed as we entered this new chapter, picturing myself moldable clay beside the man I loved, undertaking forestry together. There was only one pitfall. Menopause lurked in my future with its hormonal unknowns. And Forest Hospital had had its share of menopausal patients.

PART 4
VERMONT
1980-1992

At a crossroad, the lovers take a crucial step toward pulling together. The enemy resurfaces. White fear drives the journey toward the ordeal, the core of despair.

27

Relapse

"Can this be right?" I asked, as we turned onto a gravel road with a strange name. "Did the realtor mention anything called Buffalo Farm?"

Peter slowed a little in our rented Honda, winding through patches of woods edging former pastures with a remote house here and there. We followed directions, passing the small cemetery with a decorative iron fence our Middlebury classmate-turned-realtor had mentioned, and there it was, the red farmhouse we had seen in snapshots on his bulletin board. We were alone with the neighboring gravestones. The agents had been tied up with other clients.

We turned onto the scruffy lawn between tumbled stone walls, parked, and took a look around us. Overgrown bushes and straggly spruces bordered the road. A few twisted apple trees were dying in a remnant orchard. Weeds choked a struggling garden.

We walked toward the house with its fading paint and peeling shutters. The porch to the back door needed new floorboards. We peeked through the dining room windowpanes missing putty, distorted by waves and bubbles. Slanting floors buckled, bare of furniture. A kitchen with a sink on stilts had open shelves and a dock chimney behind a jutting stove. A door to a bathroom half hid a washbasin with two faucets.

We circled around to the north side to spy into the living area. Plaster rained off the ceiling lath onto the bare floor. The hillside was pushing the old sills off the foundation. The shed sagged. No one loved this place.

I looked at Peter, eyes and mouth wide open.

"Yes! This is it, Peter!"

I was crazy about the whole property. Here was rural, upland Vermont as rundown as "Grampy's camp," a cabin my grandfather would treat us to in Mendon, with kerosene lanterns. This farm called our names. It would pull us together. I fell in love at first sight. Peter smiled. And took charge.

"Let's get a map of the place, see a survey. It has 187 acres of woodlands, more than I had pictured." He was scanning the ragged pasture, deliberating.

This old hill farm in a hollow on the flank of the Green Mountain's Northfield Range was unpretentious, a place we could patch up that would sit lightly on our shoulders. It was 140 years old and had good bones, even if arthritic.

Without a neighbor in sight, I felt my friends would be the farmhouse itself, first, then the hills and the surrounding meadows of summer memories. Elderly aunts and uncles in their nineties would come visit along with my parents. We'd have family picnics; I'd get busy painting, sewing curtains.

Peter saw it through different eyes. His interest was the forestland surrounding the house. He'd need to learn woodland management. Here was a square of earth he could improve. We drove back to the agent's office in Rutland and made an offer. When the sale finalized in December, it changed our future overnight.

"I'd like to get started this coming summer, maybe in May. We'll want to figure out what we've bought ... consult experts. Get to know the woods." Peter's eyes sparkled. He would connect with foresters, excavators, mills, logging contractors. I focused upon identifying birds.

"Eventually, we can extend our stay until color season."

Peter could see a new life requiring longer periods working the forest.

"You mean staying until October?" I hadn't considered such a lengthy interruption in my California ties.

"Why not? Aren't we building a new chapter together, more relaxed, away from people and city hassles?"

For the first time, I had a glimmer of what older friends had shared with me: newly retired husbands disrupting their routines.

"I'll probably need a tractor and brush hog. Those fields are growing up to saplings. Did you notice the rocks everywhere? I can pry out some with a crowbar and chain with your help. Are you game?"

Rock removal? I nodded vaguely, loving his enthusiasm.

When the winter ended, we made airline reservations from Los Angeles and in late May landed in Burlington at 10 p.m. In our rental car we turned at the sign marked Buffalo Farm Rd. In fifteen minutes, we arrived at our own night-shrouded fields and the farmhouse that had stolen our hearts. It looked more dilapidated than I had remembered. A slight sprinkle fell from a low fog. Peter was excited.

"We are going to have a great time improving this place! Let's start finding our boundaries tomorrow."

We unlocked the door, stepped into the chilly kitchen, set down a bag from the gas station mini-mart and put milk into the 1940s refrigerator. The handyman down the road had turned on the electricity, water and gas. The former owners had left us just what we had requested: a wood table and two chairs, two sets of dishes, a bowl and a pan or two, and the two single beds upstairs. The burners worked. I rinsed wilted lettuce in the sink and drained it on the linoleum counter while Peter pan-fried two pre-shaped hamburgers. Each act felt ceremonial. Our pulling together as a team was about to unfold! We set up the drop-leaf table next to the dining room windows, looking out on a moonless drizzle.

Sitting down on the spindle-backed chair, I felt something happen. I was about to bite into the hamburger. Arm touching arm, I was beside my dear partner, intent on my new status as teammate. Suddenly a smell sifted up through the cracks of the floor from the basement below. It was an odor so foul that it altered my tired mind instantly.

"Do you smell that?"

"Yes. Not pleasant."

Like a phantom, the stench conjured a sudden living image. Ancient things were creeping up from "down there," from the dirt and rodent runs of the cellar hole beneath us. The rankness was so strong I saw long, white bony fingers, dead for a century, slip through the floor cracks, snaking back and forth slowly upward. I froze. These protrusions seemed bent on clutching me, pulling me with them down to the cavern below.

This vision was abnormal, and I knew it. The old distorting sickness. Uncoiling, surfacing, prickling my skin. In a wave of fear, I shuddered and lost my appetite mid-bite. Peter looked at me.

"Is everything okay?"

I said nothing. After so many years of healing, after such a long stretch of creative confidence, could the old wound be seeping? Could some mental trickster still pull me into its underworld? I felt a flashback to the overwhelming force that had led to the hospital experience thirty years earlier. It passed off but left me shaky. The mustiness, I told myself, rose from old boards and discards of settlers who had built this place. Nothing more.

Peter bit into his burger frowning. I forked at my lettuce leaves nervously, finished some of the patty and smiled thinly at him. Instinctively, I hid my panic.

We cleaned up, lugged our suitcases upstairs, made the beds with Altadena sheets and pushed their iron frames together. I wanted no gaps, no crevices. Peter was suddenly, as in our early marriage, my toehold to safety. I climbed into the bed to the right and reached for his hand. We huddled together. He was soon fast asleep, sighing rhythmically. I lay awake, every skin cell alert, reasoning with myself.

"Julie. Breathe in and out slowly. Tomorrow do some yoga postures. It will take a little time to adjust."

The next morning the sun peeked through puffs of clouds and Peter couldn't wait to get outside.

"We'd better wear our boots and waterproof jackets. If you and I know anything, it's rain and Vermont. And bring pruners."

I felt cheered. Peter was in charge, land map in hand, ordering the launching of our discovery trek into our trees to the west across the road. The forestland to our east, a huge wilderness on the steep flank, would be tackled later.

"I'll bring the binoculars I packed. Oh my gosh, Peter . . . look! There—on that lower right branch—the dead one, of that apple tree! Isn't that a bluebird?"

It was a promising sign. I had inherited a love of bluebirds from my parents. I remember as a child a tale called *The Bluebird of Happiness* by Maeterlinck. It was a mysterious, strange story. Now, for the first time, we owned land that was bluebird habitat. We had the open fields that attracted them. The male took off with a flash of brilliance. I lingered, my eyes following him into the sky. Peter, crossing the road, called, "Are you coming?"

When I caught up, we bushwhacked through a forest, impenetrable here and there, ducking jagged spurs. We came across old stone walls and piles of rocks. Peter found a rusty stone-boat runner, part of a conveyance used in winter for hauling rocks to those walls. He read the land as we pushed forward, picturing the original settler heaving boulders, growing a crop.

After a few days acquainting ourselves with the nearest town market and the hardware store, we settled into our first routine. We pushed into a thick pine grove planted by former owners. The county forester gave us several days of consultation and Peter was soon removing dead pine branches with a pruning saw. My contribution was to bring a picnic and jug of ice water to a clearing around lunchtime. Peter had found his calling. Suppers in the bare dining room continued to be tainted by the unnerving smell, nibbling a little each evening at my emotions. I clung to meditation and the sight of the bluebird.

At the mention of bluebirds, the Daemon grows stern. The Cerulean Fairy cannot be counted upon when spotting its earthly reflection.

As if on cue, the Fairy warbles, "Nearer, nearer, nearer . . . lovely, lovely, lovely . . . final, final, final."

The Daemon silences the singsong. "Careful, my friend Fairy. Peril lurks near your 'final, final, final.' Bluebirds can delight or devastate."

The Fairy flashes, retorting. "Daemon, I know bluebirds. You're as unmoving as a post!"

The Daemon stares at Cerulea.

"Is it not posts that bluebirds perch upon? You know their height; I know their weight."

In the house, looking out over the road, I found a cheerful upstairs window that had once flooded sunshine upon settlers at a spinning wheel or cradle. I began writing letters in this tiny room to dear Louise. My cheery tone so recently conveying news of plans for a yoga series on television now shifted to loneliness. Louise had retired with her husband to an early Nantucket whaler's home inherited from her parents.

"Louise, will you and Bob come visit us? I'm not sure about this Vermont decision. Seeing you might boost my spirits."

I brightened when Louise's letter said they would come for a weekend the following year. Peter was in his element, sawing methodically among his—no, I reminded myself—*our* trees. It was endless hands-on work, the father-son labor of his happy childhood.

From this window I would watch my partner start across the field, garbed in hard hat, chaps and steel-toed boots, saw in hand, shovel over his shoulder. Seeing him out that upstairs window, where I was writing letters or journaling as he headed daily across the meadow alone, triggered guilt. I tried not to be late with the picnic, but could have been beside him hauling armfuls of cut branches. He didn't need me, but he liked my company. Instead, I stood on the back porch looking for bluebirds. He built us two wooden boxes and mounted them on poles. A pair came, hung around for a day or two, then departed. Eager for my companionship, Peter joined me in my bluebird fixation. I was sinking into depression.

"*Why are you always right, Daemon, my ally?*" *The Fairy's wings give a feeble flutter.*

"*Cerulea! Stand firm. I need you now, stalwart, steady, watchful. Our Eye is crucial at this point. Do not get sidetracked by our protagonist's bluebird fixation.*"

"*You are right. It was a momentary weakness.*"

The Cerulean Fairy picks up the shuttle and sets to mending a jagged gossamer rip it caused itself.

A new pathology was nosing into me. Nesting bluebirds would become the comfort that my homesickness longed for. But dependence upon a bird's whim to decide the success or failure of our Vermont purchase was capricious. Peter became watchful for a flash of blue for my sake, his old loving pattern, but bluebirds were few in our hollow. I grew mournful, tormented by the teasing of their sudden appearances and vanishings.

Peter, whistling in contentment over his new tree-limbing vocation, would return for dinner buoyant.

"I pruned thirty-seven pines today. Up sixteen feet. I counted. Just the smaller ones that can put on enough growth to make the effort worthwhile. Clear pines have a higher value at the mill than knotty ones."

"You're climbing that old handmade ladder and dragging it from tree to tree?"

"Yup. Amazingly sturdy. Does the job."

"How many of these pines do you plan to prune? There must be a thousand of them."

Sulking, I hated my behavior. It was like my mother's at times, petty, moody. I shared my embarrassment.

"Peter, I feel ashamed of myself. Why can't I just go with you and help prune? What is the matter with me? I feel the old depression sucking all the energy out of me."

"It's all right, my dearest. Just take your time. This isn't your kind of work."

Peter's antenna was tuned to my dysfunction. We were co-dependents. He excused my behavior. I remembered the book his mother had given me, *By Love Possessed* by James Cozzens. In it everyone ruined the partner they spoiled.

By late June my parents had driven east for their summer stay at their farm in Clarendon an hour south of us. One Saturday I drove down to spend the night with them. Services at the Old Brick Church in North Clarendon were their Sunday routine. As we entered the foyer the next morning, the simple altar bore a white linen runner and two candles. Light streamed in through the stained-glass windows as we slipped into our seats on the upholstered cushion, first my father, then me, then Mother. My father clasped my hand. The hymn selections were posted on the wall over the minister's carved armchair. He gave the organist her cue.

As the first notes rang out and the congregation's feet scraped to a stand, my heart began to pound. I recognized the tune and words to one of my favorite hymns, "Open My Eyes, That I May See." I had not sung it since childhood. The next line was almost overpowering, "glimpses of truth thou hast for me." I felt a catch in my throat. "Place in my hands the wonderful key, that shall unclasp and set me free . . ." Tears began streaming. My dad reached into his pocket and handed me a large white handkerchief without glancing sideward. Mother squeezed my hand. As I tried to sing, I shook. I couldn't control my sobbing. Something was unraveling at my core. Why had I repudiated my own family roots and these nurturing living waters for a belief system halfway around the world? Why was I chanting strange Sanskrit syllables in a yogic temple?

I hadn't felt such emotion in church since before marrying. A sense of coming home was washing over me: "Voices of truth thou sendest clear, everything false will disappear." Self-Realization Fellowship suddenly appeared a foreign accretion rejecting all that was true in my native soul. I returned that evening to Peter with my world of yoga assaulted by an old familiar hymn in a Congregational Church pew between my parents.

Before we returned home at the end of that first summer, I decided to visit the village church the town of Granville shared with its neighbor Hancock. The frail pastor, whose reddish hair had not faded much, leaned on his cane while his peppy wife spotted me as one of the summer folks. She introduced me to a few of the church regulars, numbering about twenty that morning. Pastor Wayne spoke softly with words both humble and genuine.

I noticed an idle organ and spinet piano to the left of the minister. After the service I went up to him.

"You didn't have a pianist this morning."

"That is true. Our last organist, Delores, moved back to Boston. She had quite a music background and created a choir."

A moment of feeling inadequate passed; I continued. "Well, perhaps I might try playing hymns some Sunday. I would need to practice here, as we don't have a piano. I'm not a trained musician."

"Mrs. Parker, we would be grateful if you would help us out musically in the summer. In any way you would like."

I made arrangements to obtain a key and the hymn selections for the next week. Alone in the church, just God and me, I practiced my favorites. It was my own little ceremony, offering my humble skill to a sanctuary equally unpretentious. I played for the church the following Sunday. Back at our farm, I sank into melancholy.

"What exactly do you want, Julie? This Vermont farm has to work for both of us."

"I know it does. I want my part in our life together to evolve into a more giving one with you."

"But we have chosen this farm together! It wasn't just my idea."

"I know. I don't know what is upsetting me. Maybe the fact you want us to be here longer than just for a couple of months' vacation. For nearly half the year. That means finding a way I can bond and connect."

"But bond and connect with me! This place can keep us busy for the rest of our lives!"

Peter had put his finger on the problem.

"You know what, Peter . . . you have found the way you want to leave your mark on the world, to a forest that will outlast us. You're finding your way. I wonder if I'm afraid of failing."

"Failing? How?"

"Maybe failing to cross this new threshold along with you . . . of declining while you flourish." I thought of Erikson's developmental stage theory for retirees: Generativity vs. Stagnation.

Peter looked confused. He came over and wrapped me in his arms, vigorous after a day of sawing.

"You know we have to be happy together. I could never leave you behind. I think it is just taking you a little longer to find your fit."

Peter was buoyed by the sense of accomplishment tree trimming and forest improvement was giving him. Why couldn't I feel enthusiastic and supportive?

Headed home in the plane beside Peter, making eager plans for the next summer, I felt a spading at my roots. Everything was splitting in two, city life alternating with rural life, a Western religion emphasizing the *other* and an Eastern one focused upon the *self*. My own dear parents had inadvertently led me back to that childhood memory of North Woodward Congregational Church. I wouldn't give up yoga, but it was no longer *the* answer. Now, everything I had based my healing upon, a feeling of adult wholeness and confidence, was crumbling. And I was turning fifty.

28

Flaws, Defects, Failings 1982

"I'm a lie, I'm a lie, I'm a lie." A cunning taunt suddenly rose up from a sinkhole inside me with its own smell. The ritual was so ingrained in me that I could carry on my soothing imagery despite this chant causing slight nausea. We were back in our Spanish home "sanctuary" with its cathedral ceiling. I was lying on our carpeted floor in meditation mode. I alone could hear these claims of fraud within me as I led my loyal yoga friends in our first guided imagery session of the fall back in California.

Now spending long summer months in Vermont together, Peter noticed my ten-year burst of yoga-related activities burning itself out. A Pandora's box sprang open, releasing a horde of spiteful emotions. I became sour and disagreeable.

"Our relationship is like an empty teakettle. There's no steam between us."

I poked and jabbed just to rattle metal.

Peter didn't buy it. "How many men would have helped you plan that television series? Or wait while you talk with everyone as I set the dinner table? If you want to fight, I can fight too."

His gumption pleased me. "I'm just sick of my life. I don't know what I want."

"Well, you'd better figure it out pretty soon. I can go to Vermont and prune trees. That will put some space between us!"

"No, I love your company. I need you ... I'm going through something weird."

"Well, go get us a glass of wine. And by the way, I'm sick of that lasagna you've marched out for three nights. How about something different ... I'll grate cheese if you'll make a corn soufflé."

Peter and I both saw the humor of our attempts to snuff out a spat before it could get going. We were by nature conciliatory. But a new, wobbly emotional state had definitely replaced my buoyancy.

In the kitchen I got out a cutting board, grater and chunk of New York nippy cheddar. Set up on the counter next to the sink, it was a job suited for Peter's patience. I stood at the stove stirring flour into a lump of butter over low heat.

"I'm feeling a little scared."

"You? Scared? The great yogi?"

I poured milk slowly into my flour-butter paste, circling the wood spoon absently.

"Something is changing. I feel like the predictability of ten years of my life is breaking up. Like I'm heading into a major shake-up."

Peter set down the half-grated cheese piece and came over to my side.

"I'm always right here beside you, you know. Your companionship is all I want." He put his arm around my shoulder. "We have many wonderful years and projects ahead of us. Vermont, for example."

"What about Vermont?" My voice sulked.

"Well, I've been thinking about our farmhouse. It is in really bad shape, sliding off its foundation. I think we'll need to do major reconstruction work on the place next summer."

"Major work? Our little farmhouse? Oh, I hope not! It is beginning to sound like a weight on us. I like its tattered charm ..."

Peter went back to the cheese. He brought the grater and board over to the frying pan to sprinkle in the chunk all shaved, scraping the last flakes off with the edge of the grater.

"Well, we don't want it to fall into that cellar hole that gave you the creeps. Remember the article you cut out of the *Herald* about that architectural conservator working on houses in Woodstock? We might contact him."

"Oh, Woodstock! The fanciest town in Vermont! He wouldn't bother to come see our humble place."

"We don't know . . . he could at least refer us to someone . . ."

The cheese was melted. I asked Peter if he would mind whipping the egg whites while I turned off the burner, stirred in two egg yolks, opened a can of corn and added it to my soufflé mixture with a shake of onion and Worcestershire sauce. My spirits sank. The soufflé, in its 325-degree oven, rose.

"I can't bear the thought of our farmhouse getting all revamped and prettified."

Peter kept his plans to himself, sensing his wife on the verge of irrationality.

In early spring, Peter began to plan his routine for our new Vermont summers.

"I think I might need a tractor. Nothing fancy, just an old Ford model that I can attach a brush hog to for mowing our fields. It could make rock removal easier too."

Slowly I realized we were adopting the idea of living together in two separate places—Vermont and California—for two major time periods, bridging two vastly different climate zones. And we had diverging agendas. I talked to myself:

"Julie, Vermont is the land you love. You and Peter met in Vermont, and you now have your own place there. It is not only tree pruning and road ditching. Remember you saw bluebirds. There may be a nesting pair. And don't overlook the flower garden out front. It needs your attention. And your parents have a summer place an hour away. You have fun playing the piano with your mom."

"I'm scared, I'm scared, I'm scared," I chanted. I felt sick. I disappeared upstairs to our bed, filled a hot water bottle and lay down, curling around its rubbery warmth. Peter was at his desk downstairs; I hoped he wouldn't discover me.

Six weeks later we landed in Burlington's airport at 9 p.m. We drove south and turned onto our farmhouse's patch of worn grass in the black of night in our rented car. As we entered, the inescapable smell of basement rodents made me swoon. Our footsteps echoed.

"Well, here we are! Welcome to our Vermont retreat." Peter chuckled as we lugged suitcases up the creaking staircase. By nine the next morning, 6 a.m. California time, we stumbled downstairs in the chill morning air to the little bathroom. We took turns washing at the small sink with its hot and cold faucets. Dressed in what I had worn on the plane, I set our table with new dishes I had ordered over the winter. These octagonal plates and bowls, brown sprigs on shining white, looked pleasingly antique. We had a bowl of cereal, toast with a new toaster and a pot of coffee. Peter knew as we sat down by the dining room window that my eyes would turn immediately to the apple tree branches at the edge of the lawn. It was a step forward from panic at the stench in the basement. I scanned the nest boxes he had built. He looked out as anxiously as I did for signs of a bluebird.

"Julie! Look over there. Isn't that one? At the top of the tree to the left!"

Peter was right. For the next few days, I was in high spirits. We watched a male flying from box to box as his female balked. She sat on a branch unmoving. He sang louder and louder. For three days his gentle warble woke me up at 5 a.m., barely audible, through the open bedroom window. He persevered. At breakfast we watched him pick up a blade of dry grass, stick his head in one box and deposit it inside.

He disappeared entirely into the other. No go. His partner simply sat watching or flying in another direction. After a week of his failure to persuade her, the two were gone. I was heartbroken. But I could see the parallels between my behavior and the female's snubbing her partner's efforts. He had perched on posts where I could watch him until my eyes were saturated with blue. The pair was easy prey for raptors. Everything about bluebirds was fragile, distorted in my disturbed state.

"Come on, darling. Let's walk up into the woods. We'll put up more bluebird boxes. They're not so hard to make. We're sure to persuade a pair to nest sooner or later."

Peter swung a shovel over his shoulders, and I carried pruning shears. We picked up branches as we walked along, clearing the road that was barely a double-rutted trail in the grass here and there. Peter dug out remnants of ditches. His mind was thinking, planning.

"One of the first things we need to do is put in a better road up here. People say Conrad Duval is the best road builder. I'll call him later."

"Good idea." I was trying to concentrate. As we gained elevation, our trees were taller, more mature. We practiced our identifying skills. Sugar maple, soft maple, see the leaf difference? Lots of ash. A rare black cherry. White birches were always easy to spot, bark peeling off in strips like paper. We came across sheep fence, wired into rectangles the size of a post card, very different from the rusty remains of barbed wire we had spotted across the road growing into old tree trunks. There, cows formerly grazed. Stone walls meandered through our forest, proving it was formerly open land. An ovenbird's chatter followed us up the road, and we heard a unique song I learned later was the black-throated blue warbler's. We heard a wood thrush and then a hermit thrush, both songs liquid and hollow reed-like, more beautiful, I had to admit, than the bluebird's.

As we drove fifteen minutes into town to the Rochester grocery store for supplies, Peter shared something. He had called the architectural conservator to talk about a major restoration project on our house.

"You did? You found his phone number?"

"Yes. He is connected to the conservation department of the University of Vermont. I feel we have to do this."

"Well, what did he say? He probably wasn't interested in our place."

"He's coming day after tomorrow. He sounded very motivated. We have to take the bull by the horns, Julie. We can't just let this historic house collapse."

My little cabin in the mountains suddenly grew fangs.

Philip Marshall arrived right on time. He jumped out of his car and greeted us on the lawn with a smile.

"Hi, Parkers. I'm Philip and you have a nice little Greek Revival here. Do you have any idea when it was built?" He strode with us eagerly toward the kitchen porch door.

Philip's energy was contagious. As he headed for the big patch of missing plaster in the living room, I stopped him.

"Did you say our place is 'Greek Revival?' I had no idea this old farmhouse had such a fancy name."

"I can tell you when it was built, give or take a few years."

Philip got out his penknife and began digging at the exposed lath in the living room. He examined the grain and lines on the raw wood strips to determine what kind of saw the mill had used to cut the lath, circular or straight.

"About 1840. Most of these houses never had a walk-in fireplace. Franklin stoves had been invented. Nobody wanted the old smoky fireplaces any longer."

Something about our particular dwelling intrigued Philip.

"Notice the trim around your front door? And over the living room windows? Slightly V-shaped, not straight. Copying Greek temples. That was the idea. And notice the wood paneling under each one of your parlor windows? You don't see that often. There is added molding that casts a little shadow. This house was built in the vernacular, uncommonly creative."

"Vernacular? What do you mean, vernacular?"

"I mean the builder, probably a farmer, didn't have lots of money, but he had the books that were circulating in Connecticut or Boston. He followed their Greek designs with more attention to detail than the average Revival house up here in Vermont. Yours is quite unusual."

By the time Philip left, both Peter and I had new respect for our purchase. We signed him up to plan a restoration, which would guide the construction at every stage, following architectural fidelity wherever possible. My hope for upstairs dormers met with a friendly wince from Philip, pointing out the unbroken roofline as one of its major features predating dormers. Our windows were especially valuable, larger than those of most farmhouses. They needed special linseed oil and turpentine feeding.

When Philip left, we looked at each other, recognizing the magnitude of what was ahead. We would have to move out, perhaps stay at my parents' summer home in Clarendon. They usually headed back to Detroit in early August. Peter engaged a local firm that sent us to several sites to see the quality of their work.

The next day, following Philip's suggestions, Peter began gingerly removing the downstairs windows, leaving our house open to wind and rain. He found two old sawhorses in the cellar. The screeching of original, handmade nails being extracted now began. It seemed our farmhouse's eyes were being pried out. The brutal demolition of the foundation would soon begin.

By August the violation of our humble dwelling had begun in earnest. Bulldozers and excavating machines arrived and removed truckloads of rock and dirt from the shallow cellar. Trucks actually backed right into the cavern being hollowed out underneath our fragile domicile on jacks. The crew was lowering the basement two feet. Cement trucks arrived to pour concrete into wood foundation forms. When the concrete hardened, workers bolted the old beams of the house to it. They replaced rotting ones that had shifted off the old cellar hole stones at the base of the hill slope on the north side. When finished, we would have a solid basement we could stand up in, with furnace and water heater. The smell would be gone.

My feelings were roiling. Some days I felt thrilled to watch our own bit of history rise anew in the hands of master craftsmen. At other times I shivered and wanted to run away from the crashing racket of destruction. Soon the house could not be lived in; we moved for the duration of that summer to my parents' farm.

One day, driving up to inspect the progress, what I saw overcame me. Our beleaguered house, suspended on jacks, was surrounded with a moat. Boards crossed the chasm to its entry. The front door had been removed but the screen door swung forlornly in the wind letting in filth, animals, any intruder who wanted to take shelter. I had a visceral seizure; it was more violation than I could bear. Those were *my* underpinnings being ravaged. I began sobbing uncontrollably. That house had been brutalized in too many ways for me, orifices open to the elements, foundation bulldozed. I returned to my parents' farm trembling.

I continued to play the piano and sometimes even the simple organ for the church in Hancock, now practicing on my parents' old scored-varnish upright. Peter attended at times, if it was not Communion Sunday. For him, the idea of "Take the Cup," even Welch's grape juice, was heresy. He listened to me practice hymns that were surprisingly tricky in rhythm and full of sharps and flats, asking if I made that many mistakes on Sundays. I did my yoga routine in Clarendon alone, accepting a little bitterly the fact yoga was no longer the only "way."

Our farm was transforming in its own precarious rite of passage. The restoration was giving us a new kitchen, a refurbished downstairs bathroom and a spacious second one upstairs. We'd have a wood furnace in the basement, washer and dryer and lots of space for storing garden tools. A craftsman from Maine would spend the winter replastering the entire downstairs.

When the last Sunday came before our departure for California, I chose as the recessional "*God be with you 'til we meet again.*" Tears blurred the sight of my fingers. I was beginning to love this little church and its handful of non-emotive members. With promises that I would be back next year, we parted. These unassuming Vermonters were helping me find a toehold in our seasonal forestry life. Back at our farmhouse, however, where Peter continued during the day to prune the pine plantation and lay out roads with our new forester, the depression was waiting for me like a tick. It jumped onto my fragile cheerfulness that morphed into torpid moroseness.

29

Beyond Despair

"Julie! Louise's husband Bob just called. He wants to come visit us next week. To see our tree farm; to see you." Peter greeted me upon my return from watering the garden peonies to our sturdy and newly straightened farmhouse back porch. I had hoped its lovely restoration would be the antidote I longed for. Peter watched as my spirits wilted. My depression was place-specific, returning for the sixth year as we unpacked for another Vermont forestry summer, his new passion.

"Me? All the way from Nantucket? Why me?"

"Because you and Louise were so close. Maybe he hopes a visit will cheer him up."

As we had headed once again to Vermont, I had lightened a little during the bustle of packing. But two losses had recently deepened my moroseness. Both my beloved father and Louise, the one I treasured above all others except family and my friend Diane, had died. When Louise visited us the summer before, she had confided to me her leukemia diagnosis. Chagrined, I had suggested we drive to a Vespers service at the Weston Priory in south-central Vermont. There, we had joined the monks singing evensong as our voices floated through the open sanctuary into the fragrant night air. At our farm the next day, in a clearing by a giant pine near a stony intermittent brook, we had meditated. On the plane I made plans to go back, alone this year, to recapture Louise's essence under that same conifer.

The second day, after mourning the emptiness once again of our bluebird nesting boxes, I walked through the tall grass to the clearing under the great pine. Carrying a stool, trying to recall the solace of being with Louise, I suddenly crumpled. Life was too hard. My star had risen and fallen. I longed for rest. Peter might have to carry on our Vermont family forest alone. Peter's discouragement at this unshakeable gloom was as heavy as my own. I was cursed, dooming not only my own future but that of the man I loved. I was contaminating Peter.

A new terror set in, of my bleakness metastasizing. If hopelessness expanded, I would lose my will to exist, spelling the end, however that finality might manifest itself. Past episodes had been much more deadly than this new Vermont-induced melancholy. Yet this seventh setback was sinking me, wearying me the most deeply. I could function, but felt my will to do so dying.

"Daemon, we are losing her! I cannot watch this scenario any longer!"

"Cerulea, this is the time when we must stand together."

"Stand together while we watch her sink into failure?"

"What makes you assume failure?

"Listen to her! She is depleted, giving up."

"Yes, we may lose her, but watch, Cerulea. She is entering the essential period. Join **me,** not our protagonist."

The thought of Bob visiting was a distraction, but when he arrived the sight of him overwhelmed me with a rush of memories. After preparing appetizers to go with the martini Peter had mixed, dinner warming, I had to excuse myself and run upstairs. On our bed I broke down, distraught, unable to face the two men chatting below. I was losing it without a doubt, sensing something like a seizure about to erupt, trapping me in chagrin in our bedroom. I wrapped my arms across my chest and rocked frantically in place, expecting at any moment to roll to the floor in a grand mal convulsion.

Instead, something surprising happened. Louise materialized before me. Just briefly. I saw her evanescent form. But she delivered a clear and encouraging message. Her words will never leave me.

"Julie, you have a beautiful mind. Tell Bob I love him and to give my love to the children."

That was it. Then she faded. I was stunned. A beautiful *mind*, the one I felt I was about to lose? What a reassurance from some higher vantage point. It yanked me away from the abyss once again and sent me downstairs to deliver her message.

The men stopped, bemused for a moment at what I was reporting. This odd interruption jarred the two in the living room. Peter was describing our forest management plan as preparation for a woods walk the next day. Bob thanked me, silent for a moment, then returned to the conversation with Peter.

I went into the kitchen, revived, and prepared dinner for the three of us. But I kept reviewing what had just happened. If wavelengths of one's psyche are in a sufficiently disturbed state, perhaps a rare vibration from another realm, quantum mechanics stuff, may be able to penetrate through and "communicate." All I know is Neils Bohr talked about parallels between science and Eastern mysticism. This was the second time I had experienced a vision.

Bob was a master furniture maker. The next day I showed him a chair bottom I was caning. The slow weaving of thin strips of rattan palm soothed my scrambled nerves. In and out, under and over, first creating perfect little squares, then adding the diagonal canes that give the seat its strength and rows of little hexagons. It was like darning a hole in a heel, an Achilles' heel. Bob examined my work, his pipe in hand. He looked closer.

"You've done a nice job here. There is only one little problem with your diagonals. You are going under with them where you should be going over. See, look closely. This cane is catching against the two cane strips where they cross. If it went under here instead of over, it would tend to slip between the verticals and horizontals. It's not a big problem."

I felt a pleasant apprenticeship under the expertise of Louise's husband. He helped me correct my novice job with a minimum of unweaving. Peter had always liked Bob, who complimented him on the restoration work he had done on our six-over-six paned windows. Bob had restored parts of his own home in Nantucket built in the 1700s. I was sad to see him drive to the Cape Cod ferry that would chug him back to the remote island.

Mother was now alone on her Clarendon farm. She had made the courageous decision to leave Detroit and a lifetime of chosen friends to move permanently to Vermont. Traveling down to visit her was an escape from the humbling ruins of my fervor for our woods, for working beside Peter. The depression always lifted as I headed to spend a day with her.

Oddly, being a widow suited Mother quite well. She had seemed totally dependent upon her husband, always at her side, chopping celery or onions in the kitchen, locating her hearing aid, searching for her glasses or dentures, jumping to her every need. At night especially he tried, with phenobarbital pills, to calm her. She now took the helm of her life and had a series of male helpers at her beck and call. Sadly, it appeared my father had spent his life in vain.

Playing the piano together now became a major bond between my thriving parent and me. We practiced our three Mozart duets over and over at the 1920s upright. But on the way back to Granville my depression returned on cue, like a Lilliputian jeering and snickering over the string it had wound around me. At times the waves came like emotional labor pains, growing in frequency and severity.

One late afternoon, as I pulled onto the beaten grass beside our beautifully restored farmhouse, Peter waved cheerily from the shed in his chaps and hard hat. He had had a wonderful day chain-sawing three multi-trunked soft maples. He had limbed them and cut them into lengths, long ones for the wood furnace in our new basement, shorter ones for the Garrison stove in the living room.

"If we come back for a winter visit, we'll be all set. How's your mom?" His upbeat energy and resourcefulness made stark the contrast between our moods.

"You've been working hard," I mumbled.

He was now splitting the small logs with an axe, swinging it dead-eyed into the center of their four-inch diameters. The thwack of metal on wood, the cracking of the splitting fiber, the thud of the pieces landing on the ground made a percussive melody. In silence I gathered up the scattered firewood pieces and stacked some on the woodpile as he had shown me. There was an art to stacking to avoid the whole pile collapsing. But my heart wasn't in it. I went into the kitchen to prepare dinner. Peter sensed my melancholy and soon came in to help. Though it was hard to admit it, our relationship was mirroring the lopsided bond I had witnessed between my parents. Selfless, giving father. Selfish, grudging mother. Another wave of shame set in.

That night I descended to a nadir. Lying on top of our bed crosswise, I had a moment of such despair that I cried out in agony. Peter had accompanied me upstairs, equally distressed. Blurting out, I sobbed to no one in particular, to aliveness perhaps.

"I just want to die. I want to die. Let me die."

Peter's angst rose to meet mine, and clasping my shaking arm, he responded, almost shouting.

"I am going to find help for you! I'm going to call our doctor in California! You are *not* going to have to go through this any longer!"

His fervor divided the pain for the moment. A few days later a prescription for Estrogen replacement therapy arrived, thanks to our primary care physician. It helped. My emotional pain might have been partly caused by withdrawal symptoms from dying hormones, the same endocrine imbalance that had played havoc with childbirth.

A week later another depression set in, ominous, foreboding, edging toward fatality. We had just finished lunch of a peach and blueberry salad, ripe fresh fruit in season that had failed to cheer me. Peter made a suggestion.

"Why don't we take a walk through our woods to the back meadow?" We had mounted a swing the week before for our grandson in an open field at the end of our new road into the pine plantation.

"I'll push you on the swing you helped me put up for little Andy when he comes next summer."

I broke into tears.

"I can't. I haven't the energy to do anything but sit here or go upstairs. I hate what is happening to me. I hate how it is spoiling your joy, and everything you love about our farm. This terrible depression is ruining *both* of our lives."

Peter walked alone to that meadow. Consumed by my demons, I lay propped on an elbow, torturing myself by watching him out the upstairs window. At one point I saw him bend down and pick a lone daylily and carry it for a while before it slipped from his hand.

An hour later he returned. From our bedroom I could hear the sounds of his tools as he hung them in the shed. His boots dropped heavily on the back porch. The screen door creaked. His footsteps crossed through the hallway and mounted the front stairway, wearily, deliberately. I turned and lifted my head from the bed pillow. There he was, standing in the doorframe, the beautiful man I wanted to support, whose joy and passion I longed to amplify. As he approached, he looked me deeply in the eyes, then sat slowly on our bed. There was a long silence. Then he spoke. His words were filled with resignation.

"Julie, I have been thinking and thinking. I have come to a conclusion. Here it is. Maybe this Vermont farm is not for us. Maybe we are going to have to sell it. Maybe it is just not meant to be."

What? What was I hearing! In shock, I bolted upright. I studied Peter's eyes, his chest, bent in surrender. This pronouncement, confusing the cleverness of neurons locked in some long-ago, foot-stomping little girl "I won't!" retort, unshackled my prisoner-mind in an instant. Sell our farm? Give up our retirement plan? The forest that had made him happier than he had been in his entire working life?

I saw our dream, *his* dream shattering, the culmination of our life and love together. This willingness to give it all up, in a supreme effort to help me be happy, was too great a sacrifice.

Then surprising words from within, a conclusion I did not recognize, jumped out of my primal child, whispered to me alone: "Peter *does* love me more than he loves our farm!"

I recoiled. This infantile deduction was weird and totally unconscious. It framed me as being in competition with the farm for Peter's affection. Worse yet, I had won! Peter's surrender had unmasked my saboteur, the omnipotent child, the *enfant terrible*. I looked at Peter with a profound feeling of gratitude and shook my head.

"No, Peter. No."

A false barricade in my awareness began to founder. I suddenly saw the sham of what had been trapping me, terrifying me. I had tried to hide my shame over megalomania. Peter had exposed it. His selfless act had revealed me to myself, and awakened what was genuine in me, my unflinching power of insight, a willingness to acknowledge my own pathetic pettiness.

Two nights later the misery peaked. I lay in bed, feverish. I defied it. I would be Peter's companion in our farm life no matter how damaged and diminished! Images of my weary frame struck me down with vividly sensed degeneration. Creeping into every cell was Parkinson's disease. Never mind. Or was it multiple sclerosis? I tried to greet the deterioration bravely. Now I could see it was cancer, surely cancer. No. It was neurological disintegration, dementia.

I made peace with each. I would carry on beside Peter as a half-person! He deserved it, even if my entire mind and physiological system were failing under the crippling forces of menopause!

I soothed myself with a comforting little metaphor. *I will be like the old tree at the foot of our orchard. It is totally hollow inside, yet it puts out leaves and an apple or two every year.* Peter was asleep beside me, perhaps grieving for his lost dream. I continued my own mourning. *Its tiny band of cambium tissue is still alive, bringing nourishment up from its roots. I can do that for Peter. I will be his partner, no matter how damaged. I will die standing by him the way he has stood by me.* I surrendered to the erasure of all my life potential, to help him at last fulfill his.

As these crumbling images succeeded one another, a cloud of great murkiness seemed to be thinning. Something numinous was infiltrating all these states as I accepted disease after disease. The cloud was now a mist. Suddenly, the last wisps dissipated and something overpowering and brilliant was tugging me. Faster and faster. Where was I? I was now flooded with a marvelous illumination, as if passing through a crack in the shell of the Universe. Everything altered instantly—fear, affliction, despair. I was face to face with Eternity. The very same stuff that a moment earlier had been full of disease now transformed into Beneficence, Love, both personal and impersonal.

I had just experienced a healing blast of the Cosmos, a final transformation. It was so blinding a glimpse that it melted the hooks of my every flaw. Was this what all my setbacks had been driving me toward? Had all the relapses been leading to this moment, this end goal?

Suddenly I realized I'd gone through many deadly "dyings" only to find that the soul cannot perish any more than the Cosmos can end. The healing revealed Infinity at my core. From now on I would live with a beautiful duality . . . awareness of my transitory, limited, ordinary self, holding hands gently, even tongue-in-cheek, with my eternal Self.

Overpowered with gratitude that night as I lay in bed, or reverence and compassion for all existence, I thought of all the individuals who had loved me and whom I loved, those still alive, those who had served as teachers. Peter, above all. Peter's mother, my mentor Louise, my beloved father, Mother, George, who had outgrown scorn to become one of my greatest comforters, dear Aunt Ellen, so sweetly giving, Mrs. Harris, my first ideal adult, and her daughter, my enduring friend Diane. And whom could I love more than our precious daughters, part of me, like my mind that had been tortured and then restored? But I had also been ruthless at times. I had been a fierce rejecter of those who were blind, victims of their own twisted upbringings, all calling out, "Mother, love me, help me, where are you . . . Mama? Save me!" I had scorned humanity. Now I wanted to embrace every groping, miserable member of our species alive, all of us caught in webs of our own making. I had seen the enemy, and it was I.

Immediately I knew I would be well. At last I would know how to truly love and be a mature human being despite quirks. My most resistant fears had melted into butter. Life's battles were all illusion, hiding the true Reality, tucked in a fold, in the Cosmic Mystery. There I was, in bed beside the man I was in love with, my body on one plane, my consciousness on another. I had climbed to the top of that mountain, the one whose foot I had stood at in the psychiatric hospital in a hell world. Now I was seeing with the Eye that had been watching me, accompanying me, never intervening, never deserting me. I was seeing the view from the top. The Eye had become my own.

"Well, my Cerulean Fairy, my faithful ally, there you have it."

"Yes. I hardly dare say it. Our protagonist has reached . . . no, I won't say it."

"Why? You can't jinx attainment of the Final Goal." The Daemon almost smiles. *"Can we take a rest now, my Daemon friend?*

"Yes, Cerulea. Rest for now. One never knows the timing or whereabouts of our next candidate."

"One last question, Daemon: Do you suppose our protagonist will ever know we were watching her?"

"Some day, perhaps, Cerulea. Then you will have a companion in addition to me."

"Oh, you are sufficient, Daemon. You are tough, but I am used to you.."

Cerulea wipes a tear as the Daemon separates, then looks back and winks.

The rumble slowly fades until Cerulea can no longer hear or feel it reverberate.

Wings at rest, Cerulea slips into a deep smiling doze.

The next morning everything felt the same yet looked more vibrant. Awake before Peter, I slipped downstairs and ran from window to window. Sun was streaming in the six over six glass panes of the south-facing dining room, warming my shoulders. I stroked the sills and antique mullions that Peter had coated with linseed oil mix to preserve one hundred years longer. I pulled the Swiss cotton curtains aside, the ones I had made at a second-hand sewing machine the year before. The beautiful, oversized orifices welcomed the outside in, meadows and mountain skyline, three robins running and stopping on the grass, the winding brown road disappearing beyond the cemetery.

I wanted to rush outdoors and call out to the world, "Humanity! Don't worry . . . Love and Goodness are just a veil or two away, maybe several!" I opened my arms to the old apple trees, the stone walls Peter had rebuilt, the handsome wooden gate he had designed for the beauty of it.

I got out our octagonal plates and set the table. In the brand-new kitchen I made a recipe of blueberry muffins that soon floated fragrance from the oven. Peter, smelling the aroma from our electric coffee maker, descended our still-creaky stairs. He walked through the dining room across the painted wide floorboards that warped at their edges and sank a little underfoot. In the kitchen with its new Armstrong vinyl floor, he stood by our counter.

"Yummm. I smell muffins!" Peter poured milk in a pitcher and got out the butter and crabapple jelly we had made the fall before. Neither of us said anything about my transformed demeanor. We were perhaps afraid to.

"I want to walk up our woods road after breakfast. Remember the trees I put a ribbon around last year, that perfect maple and the black cherry on the overgrown side path to the brook? Let's go find them, and make sure the ribbons are still on them, so loggers will never cut those two."

"Sure." Peter did not break the spell. "And afterwards if you want, we can continue up our new road and I'll show you how Conrad Duval made us two beautiful switchbacks. Now I can drive up the incline easily on my tractor pulling the trailer."

For the next four weeks I worked beside Peter in a new way that would become my signature role in our partnership. We'd start off together, he with a handsaw and pruners, me with clippers and binoculars strapped over my shoulder. Birds fascinated me . . . some sang songs I heard over and over.

"Wait a minute, Peter . . . can you hold up a second? Do you hear that song? Look for leaf movement . . . you are so good at spotting a bird in the trees . . ."

Peter would stop, search patiently, wanting me beside him even though the broken branch needing removal was just ahead one hundred feet. Birding is a slow, stop-and-start business.

When we reached the downed branch, I lopped tops while Peter sawed the four-inch trunk into small logs. I helped him pile them next to the road to be picked up later by his tractor and trailer. Peter was happy, I was happy, constantly interrupting our progress to look for nests or listen to the ovenbird. I was beginning to bond with our trees, identifying them by their bark or leaves like a forester.

I never had another depression. I had been driven "to my own profundity" and had "broken through, at last, to unfathomable realizations" as Joseph Campbell phrased it. Then he added, "No man can return from such exercises and take very seriously himself as Mr. So-and-So."[14] It was true; Peter and I laughed and laughed at life, at ourselves, at both meaning and absurdity.

14 Joseph Campbell, The Hero With A Thousand Faces (Princeton: Princeton University Press, 1949), 385-386.

From that moment on, we followed the migratory rhythm we had struggled ten years to establish together: seven months in California near our children, five months in Vermont on our tree farm. We found new activities at home and reasons to love both traffic-choked Los Angeles and tiny Granville, where every other lone vehicle is a pickup truck. Our neighbors had the same mix of politics as our friends in California, president cursers, president worshipers.

I became a "good enough" partner. A little more grounded, I was still that high-spirited being that could have rushed past me in Paris to the lumbering green bus. Would we recognize one another now? A loose thread from her tan winter coat had looped around my imagination and snagged my memory as we passed each other. As it unraveled, I guided it, with her unknowing compliance, into this saga.

30

Demystifying Mother

"Jeannette, did I hear our instructor tell us we needed to 'go for the jugular'?"[15]

Our teacher of Family Therapy, young and overconfident, prided herself on boldly confronting issues. She had announced that we students were to write a paper on Family Secrets.

I had enrolled in a graduate degree program in marriage and family therapy at Trinity School of Graduate Studies in Orange, California. The small school, now closed, was designed for working people. We were learning about the greats who had built psychology into a respectable field, and those before Freud who had objected to torturing asylums for the insane. Dr. Benjamin Rush, close friend to both John Adams and Thomas Jefferson, had been one such pioneer.

---

15. This chapter talks about extremely personal relationships between close family members who are deceased. However, it is not inserted gratuitously but to offer a plausible explanation and compassion for a parent's imbalance and suffering. Reflecting upon this chapter deepens my affection for my mother, who endured arch anxiety and insomnia all her life. Too late, I long to embrace her with loving gratitude for the exuberance she fostered in me, often at the expense of her own self-image that might fill up an entire notebook page.

Jeannette and I, seventy-five and sixty among a group of thirty-year-olds, looked at each other, shaking our heads. Jeannette's parents were dead, leaving only a maiden aunt. She tried to protest but was brushed off. We were told we'd never make a therapist if we couldn't find someone willing to talk about our own family's secrets.

For me, that meant Mother, dear Mother, with whom I had developed a lovely new closeness in Vermont. Watching her struggle with insomnia, claustrophobia, anxiety, and continual facial tics helped me gather a hypothesis of the puzzling trauma in her early life. I planned to visit her over the Thanksgiving holiday.

The day after arriving, I asked her if I might interview her. She was stretched out on her bed reading one of her favorite *Jalna* books for the third time.

"Mumma, I have to do a paper for my Family Therapy class. Could I interview you for it?"

"What is it you need?"

"Oh, just a few questions about your childhood."

"Okay, I'll try."

The first two questions were about place and early memory. Mother rather enjoyed reminiscing. Then came a question that was surprising even to me.

"What was your mother's feeling about sex?" A silence of a second followed.

"Mumm."

The word popped out of Mother's mouth almost of its own volition. It was what she said next that gave me a sudden peek into hidden truths that had turned into pernicious insomnia.

"Oh, dear. I am really tired. I can't take any more questions."

My parent closed up, took up her book and turned her back to me. I thought of our Family Therapy teacher. She had challenged me. I would make another try. That evening I dialed the phone number of Mother's sister, Aunt Sophie.

"Hi, Aunt Sophie, this is Julie in Vermont. I'm visiting Mother for several days."

"Oh, how lovely."

"And I have been given an assignment in my Family Therapy class to ask about your early childhood in Rutland. Would you be willing to answer a few questions? Mother sort of clammed up on me."

Aunt Sophie's tone immediately changed.

"Oh, no, dear. It was not a pretty picture."

I did a double-take. Then I continued.

"But if it was not a pretty picture, shouldn't we know about it, and try to bring some closure to it?"

Aunt Sophie was clamped as tightly as Mother. "No, dear. It is not something we ever want to talk about. I can't help you."

The total rejection by the two sisters of even the tiniest peek into their past was a powerful revelation. What I had wondered about all along now developed into a plausible theory explaining Mother's nightly suffering, and something quite sordid. I sat down and wrote up my theory, never handed in, never provable. Here it is.

The mother my mother never talked about, my grandmother, was an absentee partner to her husband, the grandfather we children loved. He, having grown up in near poverty in a Green Mountain hamlet among three sibling brothers, knew nothing about girls. After medical school training at the University of Vermont in the Victorian 1890s, he married a much younger wife, my grandmother. His sexual needs may have caused her to pull away from him. At any rate, he turned to his daughter for warmth and, in time, sexual satisfaction. The marital "duty" passed from mother to daughter, along with the dominance it bestowed on her in an unhealthy triangle.

One thing is assured: Mother used her precocious sexual prowess to attract male partners. She had never experienced love without betrayal by both parents in her youngest years. When I asked her if she had fallen deeply in love with my father, her response was, "Oh, he was a great catch." She admitted on the night before my wedding, when I had asked her what one's first sexual experience is like on that night, that she and my father had enjoyed sex before marrying.

Mother's earliest source of ego strength, then, was through sex. This role, a daughter sexualized precociously, would naturally make a child devalue and resent her mother. It overwhelms me with pathos to explore such a likelihood in my own portfolio of family secrets.

But how did this early experience, swirling turbulently inside Mother when she first married, affect her young adult life as wife to my father? I believe the confusing bond of intimacy and betrayal Mother had felt with her own father got split from her new need to be a sexual partner for her husband. Now Mother began to idealize her father. Remembering the closeness they had, she longed to be back with him in summers in Vermont. Whatever anger or distrust she must have felt for her transgressing father was now transferred to her husband, for whom she continued to use her sexuality for duty, enjoyment, and power. But I believe that every sexual act Mother engaged in mingled inextricably five feelings: dominance, disdain, pleasure, anger, and guilt. This deadly combination led to lifelong symptoms: insomnia, plunging mood at dusk, claustrophobia and facial tics that drove her to frenzy at times. The demon surfaced every evening as my father returned from work.

Coming to these conclusions, which can never be proven but which explain the desperateness I grew up with in a way no other hypothesis fits so well, gives me even greater compassion for the woman who bore me. I admire the strength she had to try to avoid, for her children, a repetition of her own life's shame and suffering. It came out in feral ways she had no control over. It led to male worship at one moment, male contempt the next. It could not help but affect us children, along with the genes we inherited from the pool of humanity. By avoiding insight, or blocking it, Mother chose, unconsciously, to suffer hidden, lifelong symptoms rather than risk the dread of facing them, surrendering to the abyss of self-confrontation which might lead in time to freedom. All sane people would make that choice.

Luckily, sexuality is not the major part of most lives indefinitely. My parents had what looked to observers like a highly compatible marriage. They loved the countryside of New England, they loved their joint relatives, they loved birding and took ice skating lessons into their eighties, as well as summer strolls to pick blackberries and identify wildflowers. They had loyal friends, and their own little reservoir of giggles. My father had the Ford Hospital.

For Mother, what can I say was her main devotion? Two years before she died, she wailed one day, "Oh, how I miss Father." She was highly intelligent, interested in all that her father loved . . . astronomy, mountain climbing, birds, his prize garden of June peas and August corn, early photography. But Mother was too damaged to develop her fine gifts more than superficially. Her lifelong friends were caught in her orbit, myself included. When I had to leave after a too-brief visit, she would cling to me and quote, like Jacob wrestling with an angel, "I will not let Thee go unless Thou bless me."[16] Mother ensnared me with irresistible flattery. She played the piano well and could read books in French, Spanish, German and Italian. Her recitations of poetry or Biblical passages revealed an unusually sharp memory.

I want to honor my mother for the fantasy she fostered in me as a child. Perhaps, although I adored my father who seemed the quiet sufferer, it was really Mother who gave me my exuberance for living. She kept me believing as long as she could. And she nudged me into the

16. Genesis 32:26 (King James Version).

limelight, to create a little charmer. Let us leave certain tangles for the Daemon. If we live again, in some strange way through our DNA and consciousness evolving throughout eternity, all may end as a flawless silken thread, without a single snag or snarl.

Epilogue

No two of us will ever experience illness in the same way or produce identical symptoms. We humans are unique despite our rubber stamp contours . . . two arms, two legs, etc. Inside, our thoughts and feelings are catalogs of such infinite influences that it is amazing we communicate at all with one another. Whether we are diagnosed with cancer, psychosis, or another life-altering disorder, its particular outline will fit no one but us.

The belief that we can share and be enriched by each other's experience, however, is the reason I have recorded this narrative. If my struggle with hidden character flaws blocking healing can inspire even a handful of sufferers to tackle their buried shames and misconceptions, my tale will have met its goal. Like Pogo, I have seen the enemy.

The nature of this enemy, which, for me, is plural, is extremely cunning. My hidden ego defenses, formed very early to survive the collective blow that I had rivals and was not omnipotent, were an ingrained part of me, like my appendix. Are any of us aware of our appendix? My attempt to understand these defenses, let alone perform a "defensectomy," was almost impossible, despite the most effective techniques of psychotherapy. While off and on in counseling and study groups I felt I was getting closer to the truth of what was causing dysfunction, those little deep-seated parts of me were hiding smugly in the marrow of my bones.

Therapy, however, definitely helped lead me to the edge of this hidden realm. At some point, in my case, on the threshold of despair, the power of insight, of stalking the wily foe using its own ruses, came into its own. I became alert to telltale utterings, behaviors, signs (like scat!) that I was getting closer to what was holding me hostage. It felt as though the entire Universe was whipping and lashing me toward an ordeal that would decree final destruction or transformation. I was trapped by my own legendary quest for the meaning of it all. When I read Christopher Vogler's mythic structure for writers, outlining the stages of the hero in his *The Writer's Journey*, (the definitive screenwriter's guide for filmmakers), I recognized myself on that dread path. From the first inciting incident one runs from, to its return until it is faced, to tests, allies, and setbacks, and finally the approach to the "innermost cave" of torment before apotheosis, I could trace the arc of my illness.

Unfortunately, for those with recurring symptoms after a major psychotic episode, looking inward for its causes is less valued than external factors: diagnosis and medication. To identify a disorder, psychiatrists go to exhaustive lengths to settle upon the right treatment plan. Diagnoses are nearly infinite. They all depend upon the DSM, the Diagnostic and Statistical Manual of Mental Disorders, the mental health provider's tome in use for over forty years, now in its fifth edition.

My first signs of serious illness, however, emerged in the 1950s, long before the DSM had gained acceptance. Psychiatric hospitals like the small private institution where I spent five months closed as the promise of new drugs expanded. Unlike large state asylums, these private hospitals had served disturbed individuals whose stays were temporary and who, I assume from the number of fellow patients I saw arrive and depart during my long stay, were likely to return to normal functioning. For me, that small haven on the banks of the Des Plaines River was a refuge where I was given a bed and meals and the time I needed to recover. If I were to suffer a recurrence of those same psychotic symptoms in today's mental health system, would there be a place for me to heal slowly, reknitting a ravaged psyche?

But what *was* my diagnosis, friends often ask. Familiar with the DSM from my graduate studies in the 1990s, I could find more or less accurate names for each of my recurring relapses as their presenting symptoms changed. The first onset on the ship was a Depersonalization Disorder, "characterized by a feeling of estrangement from one's self." The second, "Delusional Disorder," came upon me after Diane's birth, when I had visual hallucinations "with poor psycho-social functioning." The third, needing hospitalization, was "Major Depressive Disorder with Severe Psychotic Features" after childbirth. Recurring setbacks after that five-month stay exhibited a variety of unexplainable psychic "happenings" that fit loosely into "Somatoform Disorders." The final, decade-long relapse was a "Depressive Situational Disorder" that returned each summer in Vermont, influenced by the hormonal chaos of menopause.

Would I have healed in today's system of short hospital stays had I been given medications for these diagnoses? Perhaps. If so, might this quick solution have stabilized me, but impeded my long, tedious journey toward the ageless imperative: Know Thyself? Who can say? I was not a psychotic with anosognosia, a term describing the many sufferers of schizophrenia or psychosis who are unaware they are ill. These are the unfortunates who have little control over behavior and who can end up repeatedly in the criminal justice system. The prognosis is poorer for this group than it is for those like me, who know their mental cohesion has unraveled, and are terrified.[17]

---

17. Dr. Xavier Amador's book, I Am Not Sick, I Don't Need Help! (New York: Vida Press, 2012), gives an excellent account of this population.

The hyper awareness that I was losing my sanity surely increased suffering in the short run. But in the long run, the power of insight, fostered by my determination to search for the key to healing, along with an extraordinary partner, were the boons that led to my exceptional permanent wellbeing.

One particular leap of perception was more important than any other on my path to healing. It was the decision openly to consider the unexplainable, the "unscientific." Skepticism had been deeply embedded in me, promoting pride in my power of reason, and prejudice against any theory failing solid evidence. Only gradually did I realize skepticism is in part a primitive protective mechanism developed early in childhood to make up for idealism lost (Julie, it's your parents wrapping all that stuff up, dummy). In my case, I armored myself. A hidden part of me grew tough with disillusionment. I scoffed, along with many academics, at irrational ideas and thinkers on the fringe whose theories later can gain them recognition as candidates for a Nobel prize.

The agent of change for me was Nadia, my Spanish classmate whose badgering pushed against my scorn for the irrational, the "magical." Could I dare to stretch, to trust, to believe "in Santa Claus" again? Suddenly, exciting and plausible possibilities about what is real and unreal, and what might be contributing to my illness opened up new avenues of introspection. I took a step away from skepticism. Which brings up the existence of the Daemon and the Cerulean Fairy.

I do not know where they came from. The twosome materialized in the course of this story unexpectedly. Though neither intervened, their Eye-like presence in this tale is a type of intervention, their purpose hardly hidden in their constant reference to a Final Goal. Most puzzling is why my imagination split this Eye into two distinct voices, one unbending, patient, the other fluttery, eager for premature signs of "all's well." Perhaps duality is inseparable from unity.

The student that I once was in Paris did not dissolve into the void. I reach out to her in gratefulness for the agony she faced, and what it has taught me through her. She still exists in me, as youth persists in dreams and longings in all of us. Endings are not as startling as beginnings. The brilliant blue Cross, blinding me with its radiance when first painted by Diane in my meditation alcove, no longer shimmers. Time has scored its surface into a thousand blue-gray mosaics. I often forget it is there, hiding behind the covering of an old slatted Japanese calendar. It does not matter. Let our lives be painted over by newcomers who will replace us in our homes when we leave this Earth. Nothing can erase the lessons we have garnered from the Cosmos.

Acknowledgments

Over a decade ago, the juice of an idea that I had a story worth telling jelled at the Omega Institute. Our fiery leader, poet Marge Piercy, boiled into us the main ingredient of author success: grab readers in the first paragraphs or lose them. Scar tissue from that workshop toughened me just enough to bring a book to fruition. Endless companions since have traveled the journey with me.

To start, I want to thank my two wonderful California writing buddies Deborah Mindry, Cultural Anthropologist, and Susan Cross, Licensed Psychologist. With their unique insights into its meaning, they offered this story the valuable criticism, enthusiasm and faith that helped squire it toward publication. In this last process, Vermonter Rebecca Burgee, Librarian, friend and soul sister, has overwhelmed me recently with her generous outreach and assistance. Together we have visited libraries, bookstores and psychology professors; in my absence she continued alone. These three women are etched into my heart.

On monthly Thursdays, the writing group of All Saints Church in Pasadena listened many an evening to suggest more show and less tell to improve chapters. The regulars who offered encouragement were numerous, especially Bernice Fong, Kres Mersky, Drew Katzman,

Cheyenne Wilbur, Chad Michael and Elizabeth Converse. Developmental editor Margaret Diehl read my manuscript twice, helping me cut it down to satisfy agent Paul Levine. And Los Angeles agent Ken Sherman was drawn enough either to the story or to our coincidental Vermont connection to ask for five chapters. Neither worked out. Not every lottery can promise a winning ticket like the one that led me to Peter.

Vermont author Ron Powers, New York agent Katharine Sands and Pasadenan Colleen Dunn Bates, retired founder of Prospect Park Books, all surprised me with their expressions of confidence in this story's potential. NAMI (National Alliance on Mental Illness) affiliates Kristina Petter and Jodi Girouard in Burlington, Vermont, and Wayne and Lucy Meseberg, Linda Strassle, and Sylvia Gil in Greater Los Angeles, have shown strong support.

Owners Wendy Chen of Callisto Tea House in California and Anni Mackay of Big Town Gallery in Vermont hosted readings long before the book launch, as did Dr. Mark Baker, Clinical Psychologist, inviting me to speak to a large group of psychotherapists and interns at his La Vie Counseling Center in Pasadena where I was supervised upon obtaining my master's degree.

Offering technical help in Vermont, David Darr of Darrad Computer Services rescued my ineptitude at anything beyond Microsoft Word while Harlen Houghton, Vermont artist, writer and entrepreneur, helped me with Google and the endless non-story pages that make up a book. In the Los Angeles area, master printer and computer expert Ryan Tomaz, proprietor of Nationwide Litho, filled exactly the same role as David. Ryan printed a small chapbook, *The Yoke*, of the first chapters, hundreds of which I have distributed to create anticipation for *Journey Beyond Despair*.

A host of longtime California friends cannot possibly know how much their friendship and interest in my saga has meant to me: Lilo

Kilstein, Milt Hall, Dick and Judy Rubin, Ruth Judkins, Mary Cannon, Callie Shively, Richard Harvey, Fanny Adnitt, Grace Bernal-Gutglueck, Susan Bosch, Sharon Calkin, Boualem Bousseloub, Ava Liversidge and Carol Jean Rose. Many of these just named were longtime members of my yoga sessions or French classes, Ava only ten years old at the time. Tria Reed stands out for the almost sacred closeness we have had from years together enjoying spontaneous movement.

Three League of Women Voter friends, all of us committed to fossil-fuel reduction, have been especially supportive: Kitty Kroger, Cynthia Cannady and Kathy Kunysz. Daniel Henry-Smith of Siren Arts Productions has made his filming and audiovisual expertise available to me repeatedly, most recently recording with his partner Paco Silva a book session I participated in sponsored by Light Bringer Project.

In Vermont, an equally numerous group of comrades—birder Pat Folsom, Tracy Winn and husband Joe, Brad Winn and wife Colleen, Marnie Wikel, Norm Arseneault, Valerie Becker, Ron and Chris Millard, Clare Walker Leslie, David and Julia Hall, Carrie Turnbull and her sister-in-law Debbie— stopped by over and over to learn how the book was coming.

Three special individuals, one in Russia and two in France, are cherished as family extensions. Professor Emeritus Yulia Gippenreiter, former head of the Psychology Department of Moscow State University in the Soviet Union era, and I met when the Berlin Wall came down. In back and forth Moscow-U.S. visits, she has inquired often about my book's progress. Nicole Amalric, whom I met when her husband François was a visiting scholar at California Institute of Technology in cancer research, is truly a part of my deepest affection, living in Toulouse. I can bare my soul to her when we are together; she is eager to read *Journey* in French. Docteur Philippe de Wailly is part of my life history, from that student year spent in France. He has encouraged me to write and will read it if he lives a few more months, now aged 97.

Searching as long as I dared at my age for an agent and traditional press, I encountered the wonderful Steve Harrison team at Author Success, unique in guiding writers through the complexities of self-publishing and on to the more challenging stage of book promotion. Coach Cristina Smith, copy editors Valerie Costa and Beth Volz, book designer Christy Day and magnetic Steve Harrison above all have shown endless patience and guidance while urging completion of each step.

Most enduring, of course, has been the loving support of Peter, our daughters, our sons-in law, my youngest brother Charlie and wife Kathy, nieces Heather and Camille, our grandchildren and their spouses and my cousin Agnes. Cousin Jean warms my heart as well. Many read through edit after edit and gave me the best advice of all: don't preach, just tell the story. They are my faithful teachers that have made life worth living.

About the Author

A graduate of Middlebury College in 1954 with classes abroad at La Sorbonne, Julie Howard Parker has taught French and English and has been a journalist for a California weekly newspaper. An early teacher of yoga, she led sessions for forty years and dipped into commercial television classes, finding eastern philosophy compatible with her white-steepled church roots. Obtaining an MA in Marriage & Family Therapy in 1992 she created a ten-year teen relationships program serving hundreds in the Pasadena public schools.

Most important to the author has been overcoming severe mental illness and nurturing an extraordinary marital relationship with Peter. Chronicling this life story has led to a theory about mental illness as 'heroic journey.' Among her favorite books are Joseph Campbell's *The Hero with a Thousand Faces*, Viktor Frankl's *Man's Search For Meaning* and Christopher Vogler's *The Writer's Journey*.

TO LEARN MORE

Readers: Could your life be trying to tell you its story?

To explore the idea that you are the protagonist of an untold story rich with meaning please go to my website, juliehowardparker.com, and click on the link You in the main menu bar.

The questions asked may guide you to see a pattern in your personal life events: significant people, special places, longings, challenges, hardships, blessings, note-worthy periods and transitions that hold greater import than you realize.

Follow the prompts to submit your completed questionnaire and we may choose to interview you about your particular responses. We are planning a podcast. It will shine light on human life as a 'mythic-heroic journey,' following Christopher Vogler's Twelve Stages in his *The Writer's Journey*, the film 'bible' for screenwriters hoping their scripts will be considered.

There is no avoiding our "life task" as Dr. Viktor Frankl called it in his famous *Man's Search For Meaning*. We exist, things happen, we make choices, we learn, we die. Frankl, an eminent professor of psychiatry, believed, based upon his three years at Auschwitz and other Nazi prisons, that "mental health is based on tension. . . the gap between what one is and what one should become." *

*Frankl, Viktor E., *Man's Search For Meaning*, Pocket Books, Beacon Press, 1972, 165-166